P9-DBT-193

1998 SUPPLEMENT

SEXUALITY, GENDER, AND THE LAW

by

WILLIAM N. ESKRIDGE, JR.
John A. Garver Professor of Jurisprudence
Yale Law School

NAN D. HUNTER
Associate Professor of Law
Brooklyn Law School

NEW YORK, NEW YORK
FOUNDATION PRESS
1998

COPYRIGHT © 1998

By

FOUNDATION PRESS
All rights reserved

ISBN 1–56662–705–2

 *TEXT IS PRINTED ON 10% POST
CONSUMER RECYCLED PAPER*

ACKNOWLEDGMENTS

This Supplement updates the casebook through July 1, 1998.

The authors gratefully acknowledge the assistance of the following persons in the preparation of the Supplement: Sharon McGowan, Harvard Law School Class of 2000; Margaret McWilliams, Harvard Law School Class of 1999; Golda Lawrence of Brooklyn Law School; Mabel Shaw and Karen Summerhill of the Georgetown University Law Center Law Library.

*

TABLE OF CONTENTS

v

*

TABLE OF CASES

Principal cases are in bold type. Non-principal cases are in roman type. References are to Pages.

xi

*

1998 SUPPLEMENT

SEXUALITY, GENDER, AND THE LAW

*

CHAPTER 1

The Constitution and Sexuality

SECTION 2

State Regulation of Sodomy

Page 55. Add at the end of Note 3:

State appellate courts continue to reach mixed decisions on the constitutionality of sodomy statutes. The Montana Supreme Court found that the state's same-sex-only sodomy law was unconstitutional as a violation of the state constitution's right to privacy. *Gryczan v. Montana*, 942 P.2d 112 (Mont.1997). Because the statute was unconstitutional on this basis, the court declined to consider whether the law was also unconstitutional as a violation of equal protection. By contrast, the intermediate appeals court in Kansas found that its same-sex-only law was valid. *City of Topeka v. Movsovitz*, No. 77,372 (Kan.App.1998) (unpublished). The Kansas court held that the state's right of privacy extended no further than that of the federal Constitution as interpreted in *Bowers v. Hardwick*, and that the state's interest in protecting morality satisfied rational basis review, which was all that was required under *Romer v. Evans*. Meanwhile, the state of Rhode Island repealed its sodomy law in 1998.

Page 72—Add the following:

Washington v. Harold Glucksberg, 117 S.Ct. 2258 (1997); Dennis Vacco v. Timothy Quill, 117 S.Ct. 2293 (1997). The Supreme Court unanimously rejected substantive due process (*Glucksberg*) and equal pro-

1

tection (*Quill*) challenges to laws prohibiting "assisted suicide" by doctors and other potential aiders of euthanasia. **Chief Justice Rehnquist**'s opinion for the Court in *Glucksberg* set forth a conservative statement of the right to privacy line of cases. "In a long line of cases, we have held that, in addition to the specific freedoms protected by the Bill of Rights, the 'liberty' specially protected by the Due Process Clause includes the right to marry, *Loving*; to have children, *Skinner*; to direct the education and upbringing of one's children, *Meyer*; *Pierce*; to marital privacy, *Griswold*; to use contraception, *id.*; *Eisenstadt*; to bodily integrity, *Rochin v. California*, 342 U.S. 165 (1952); and to abortion, *Casey*. * * * But we 'ha[ve] always been reluctant to expand the concept of substantive due process because guideposts for responsible decisionmaking in this unchartered area are scarce and open-ended.' " [*Collins v. Harker Heights*, 503 U.S. 115, 125 (1992).] * * *

"Our established method of substantive-due-process analysis has two primary features: First, we have regularly observed that the Due Process Clause specially protects those fundamental rights and liberties which are, objectively, 'deeply rooted in this Nation's history and tradition,' [*Moore v. City of East Cleveland*, 431 U.S. 494, 503 (1977) (plurality opinion of Justice Powell) (casebook, p. xliv)], and 'implicit in the concept of ordered liberty,' such that 'neither liberty nor justice would exist if they were sacrificed.' *Palko v. Connecticut*, 302 U.S. 319, 325 (1937). Second, we have required in substantive-due-process cases a 'careful description' of the asserted fundamental liberty interest. [e.g., *Reno v. Flores*, 507 U.S. 292 (1993).] Our Nation's history, legal traditions, and practices thus provide the crucial 'guideposts for responsible decisionmaking,' *Collins*, and direct and restrain our exposition of the Due Process Clause." For example, the common law's protection of an individual's right to receive medical treatment only if she consents was found dispositive in suggesting a liberty interest in *Cruzan* (casebook, p. xlv), and the Chief Justice distinguished the alleged right to die on the ground that both common law and statutory law had long regulated both suicide and assisting suicide.

Justice Souter, concurring in the Court's judgment, set forth a "living tradition" understanding of the right to privacy, drawing from Justice Harlan's *Poe* dissent (casebook, pp. 10–12). Justice Souter explicitly analogized this to the common law method of analogy and case-by-case evolution, with this difference: unlike common law, constitutional law can proceed only cautiously, for it takes an issue away from the political process, and only when the Court is certain that a statutory policy unreasonably burdens traditionally recognized liberty interests. "It is only when the legislation's justifying principle, critically valued, is so far from being commensurable with the individual interest as to be arbitrarily or pointlessly applied that the statute must give way. Only if this standard points against the statute can the individual claimant be said to have a constitutional right." Under this standard, Justice Souter believed a constitutional right premature and that the interests identified by the state were "commensurable" to the restriction on liberty imposed by the statutes in the cases presented. [Chief Justice Rehnquist's opinion, joined by five Justices, specifically rejected the *Poe* approach to substantive due process and refused to read *Casey* to require that methodology.]

Four other Justices wrote concurring opinions. The key opinion was that of **Justice O'Connor**, who joined the Chief Justice's opinion (giving him five votes) and also wrote separately to say that the cases before the Court did not settle "the narrower question whether a mentally competent person who is experiencing great suffering has a constitutionally cognizable interest in controlling the circumstances of his or her imminent death." (The parties agreed that such a person had the right and opportunities to obtain pain-killing medications, even if they caused unconsciousness or even hastened death.) As we all know that we shall face death but cannot know the circumstances of it, Justice O'Connor was confident that the democratic process would reach suitable accommodations between "the interests of terminally ill, mentally competent individuals who would seek to end their suffering and the State's interests in protecting those who might seek to end life mistakenly or under pressure." **Justices Ginsburg** and **Breyer** joined her concurring opinion except insofar as it joined the opinion of the Court, and **Justice Stevens** expressed similar views, as had **Justice Souter** (to a lesser extent).

Quaere: Note the Court's closeting of both *Hardwick* and *Roe v. Wade*. Although the Chief Justice's opinion followed the *Hardwick* historical approach, *Hardwick* was never cited in any of the lengthy opinions in the right to die cases. Only Justice Souter cited and relied on *Roe*. Note how Justice Harlan's conservative, antigay *Poe* dissent has now become the most civil libertarian position on the current Court. How do these different developments cut in connection with the fate of *Hardwick*? Of other possible extensions of the right of privacy to criminal rules against adultery, fornication, and sexual solicitation?

The Court continued its methodological debate in *County of Sacramento v. Lewis*, 118 S.Ct. 1708 (1998), which rejected a substantive due process challenge to reckless but unintentional police action which caused the death of a citizen. **Justice Souter's** opinion for the Court applied his *Glucksberg* methodology and found that such police action was not so arbitrary as to "shock the conscience," *Rochin v. California*, 342 U.S. 165, 172–73 (1952). **Justices Scalia** and **Thomas** objected that this approach was rejected in *Glucksberg*; Justices O'Connor and Kennedy said it was not. (**Chief Justice Rehnquist**, the author of *Glucksberg,* wrote a noncommital concurring opinion.)

OTHER CONSTITUTIONAL STRATEGIES FOR CHALLENGING STATE REGULATION OF SEXUALITY AND GENDER

PART A. SEX DISCRIMINATION

Page 92—Add the following after Note 3:

4. *VMI: The Aftermath.* The 1997–98 academic year was the first at VMI to include female cadets. At its end, according to one press report, "VMI has survived women, and 23 women have survived VMI." Despite numerous complaints early in the year that the women's presence caused the first-year initiation process to be unduly softened, "the Rat Line got harsher and eventually was as intense as in past years. * * * 'The Rat Line was more physical than 90 percent of the Rat Lines I've observed,' according to the commandant of cadets. 'The rat mass is more militarily prepared and better-trained than others I've seen.'* * *'After a while, you're not thinking female rat, you're just thinking rat,' said senior Jon Spitzer, president of the Rat Disciplinary Committee." Peter Finn, "Women Reach Rat Finish Line," *The Washington Post*, March 17, 1998.

Lorelyn Penero Miller v. Madeline K. Albright, 523 U.S. __, 118 S.Ct. 1428, 140 L.Ed.2d 575 (1998). The Supreme Court rejected a challenge to a federal statute that accorded American citizenship automatically, upon birth, to a child born out-of-wedlock in a foreign country to an American mother, but denied citizenship to such a child whose only American parent was her father, unless a paternity decree was entered before the child turned 18. 8 U.S.C. § 1409(a)(4). The government defended the sex discrimination, in part, on the ground that the child's link to the mother was obvious by virtue of the birth itself, but the child's relationship to the father might be unknown until much later. Although the Court's result could have rested upon earlier decisions allowing the state some leeway in requiring fathers but not mothers to establish parental relationships, e.g., *Lehr v. Robertson*, 463 U.S. 248 (1983), the case elicited a lively debate among the Justices about whether the gender classification was a remnant of overboard stereotypes, and no one opinion or reason commanded a majority of the Court. Six Justices rejected Miller's challenge, but only two of those (**Stevens** and **Rehnquist**) found that the gender distinction survived equal protection review. Two Justices (**O'Connor** and **Kennedy**) believed that plaintiff had no standing, but said in dicta that the law was discriminatory. Two others (**Scalia** and **Thomas**) believed that the judiciary had no power to confer citizenship. Three (**Souter, Ginsburg, Breyer**) dissented on the ground that the law failed the heightened scrutiny test. Thus, five Justices agreed that it violated the Equal Protection Clause. The following excerpts will give you a flavor of the split among the Justices.

Justice Stevens delivered the judgment of the Court but wrote a plurality opinion joined only by himself and **Chief Justice Rehnquist**. He was mindful of the Court's admonitions that statutes resting upon gender stereotypes must be subjected to searching scrutiny but found that the statute was based upon a neutral state goal of ensuring reliable proof of parenthood (*Lehr*). "Section 1409(a)(4) is not concerned with either the average father or even the average father of a child born out of wedlock. It is concerned with a father (a) whose child was born in a foreign country, and (b) who is unwilling or unable to acknowledge his paternity, and whose child is unable or unwilling to obtain a court paternity adjudication. A congressional assumption that such a father and his child are especially unlikely to develop a relationship, and thus to foster the child's ties with this country, has a solid basis even if we assume that all fathers who have made some effort to become acquainted with their children are as good, if not better, parents than members of the opposite sex."

"Nor does the statute assume that all mothers of illegitimate children will necessarily have a closer relationship with their children than will fathers. It does assume that all of them will be present at the event that transmits their citizenship to the child, that hospital records and birth certificates will normally make a further acknowledgment and formal proof of parentage unnecessary, and that their initial custody will at least give them the opportunity to develop a caring relationship with the child. Section 1409(a)(4)—the only provision that we need consider—is therefore supported by the undisputed assumption that fathers are less likely than mothers to have the opportunity to develop relationships, not simply, as Justice Breyer contends that they are less likely to take advantage of that opportunity when it exists. These assumptions are firmly grounded and adequately explain why Congress found it unnecessary to impose requirements on the mother that were entirely appropriate for the father. * * * The biological differences between single men and single women provide a relevant basis for differing rules governing their ability to confer citizenship on children born in foreign lands."

Justice O'Connor, joined by **Justice Kennedy**, concurred in the Court's judgment, on the ground that the daughter (the claimant for citizenship) did not have third-party standing to raise the constitutional issues presented by the discrimination against her father (the American citizen already). "Although I do not share Justice Stevens' assessment that the provision withstands heightened scrutiny, I believe it passes rational [basis] scrutiny for the reasons he gives for sustaining it under the higher standard. It is unlikely, in my opinion, that any gender classifications based on stereotypes can survive heightened scrutiny, but under rational scrutiny, a statute may be defended based on generalized classifications unsupported by empirical evidence. See *Heller v. Doe*, 509 U.S. 312, 320 (1993)." **Justices Scalia** and **Thomas** concurred in the judgment on the ground that "the Court has no power to provide the relief requested: conferral of citizenship on a basis other than that prescribed by Congress."

Justice Ginsburg's dissenting opinion, joined by **Justices Souter** and **Breyer**, responded with the anti-stereotyping rationale for heightened scrutiny illustrated by *Craig v. Boren* (casebook, p. 80) and the VMI Case (pp. 81–90). As she had done in her VMI opinion, Justice Ginsburg engaged in a careful examination of the history of the provision, the assertedly stereotypical assumptions that gave rise to it, and the nongendered rules that would serve the government's stated purposes. "The section rests on familiar generalizations: mothers, as a rule, are responsible for a child born out of wedlock; fathers unmarried to the child's mother, ordinarily, are not. The law at issue might have made custody or support the relevant criterion. Instead, it treats mothers one way, fathers another, shaping government policy to fit and reinforce the stereotype or historic pattern. Characteristic of sex-based classifications, the stereotypes underlying this legislation may hold true for many, even most, individuals. But in prior decisions the Court has rejected official actions that classify unnecessarily and over broadly by gender when more accurate and impartial functional lines can be drawn."

Justice Breyer's dissenting opinion, joined by **Justices Souter** and **Ginsburg**, responded that the statutory discrimination was not narrowly tailored to the plurality opinion's rationale, also inconsistent with *Craig* and with the fundamental nature of the parent-child and citizenship interests involved: "[A]ssume that the American citizen is also the Caretaker Parent. The statute would then require a Male Caretaker Parent to acknowledge his child prior to the child's 18th birthday (or for the parent or child to obtain a court equivalent) and to provide financial support. It would not require a Female Caretaker Parent to do either. The gender-based distinction that would impose added burdens only upon the Male Caretaker Parent would serve no purpose at all. Second, assume that the American citizen is the Non–Caretaker Parent. In that circumstance, the statute would forgive a Female Non–Caretaker Parent from complying with the requirements (for formal acknowledgment and written promises to provide financial support) that it would impose upon a Male Non–Caretaker Parent. Again, the gender based distinction that would impose lesser burdens only upon the Female Non–Caretaker Parent would serve no purpose. * * * [W]ere Congress truly interested in achieving the goals Justice Stevens posits in the way Justice Stevens suggests, it could simply substitute a requirement of knowledge-of-birth for the present subsection (a)(4); or it could distinguish between caretaker and non-caretaker parents, rather than between men and women. A statute that does not do so, but instead relies upon gender-based distinctions, appears rational only * * * if one accepts the legitimacy of gender-based generalizations that, for example, would equate gender and caretaking—generalizations of a kind that this Court has previously found constitutionally impermissible.''

PART B.   SEXUAL ORIENTATION DISCRIMINATION

Page 108—Add the following before Problem 1–3:

NOTES: WHAT CONSTITUTIONAL PRINCIPLE DOES *ROMER V. EVANS* STAND FOR?

1. *What Was Wrong with Amendment 2?* Academic theories of *Evans* have proliferated. Consider some theories of what was "constitutionally wrong" with the Colorado initiative:

(a) it deprived gay people of the right to participate equally in the political process;[a]

(b) the law was a denial of the "equal protection of the laws" in the most literal sense, as it closed off state process to one vulnerable group;[b]

(c) the law may not draw moral distinctions based upon sexual practices between consenting adults (therefore strongly inconsistent with *Hardwick*);[c]

(d) the state cannot, without justification, single out one social group for "pariah" status,[d] or the state has an obligation to remedy

---

a. This was the theory followed by the Colorado Supreme Court, *Evans v. Romer*, 854 P.2d 1270 (1993), (casebook, pp. 727–29), and has been endorsed as essentially the Court's theory, notwithstanding the Court's refusal even to mention it. See Pamela Karlan, "Just Politics? Five Not So Easy Pieces of the 1995 Term," 34 *Houston L. Rev.* 289, 296 (1997); Nicholas Zeppos, "The Dynamics of Democracy: Travel, Premature Predation, and the Components of Political Identity," 50 *Vand. L. Rev.* 445 (1997), as well as Caren Dubnoff, "*Romer v. Evans*: A Legal and Political Analysis," 15 *L. & Inequality* 275 (1997) (this is the theory the Court should have adopted).

b. Brief by Laurence Tribe et al., *Evans*, the so-called "Scholars' Brief" filed in the case.

c. Robert H. Bork, *Slouching Towards Gomorrah: Modern Liberalism and American Decline* 112–14 (1996) (disapproving); Ronald Dworkin, "Sex, Death, and the Courts," *N.Y. Rev. Books*, Aug. 8, 1996, at 49 (approving); William Eskridge, Jr., "*Hardwick* and Historiography," 1998 *U. Ill. L. Rev.* (cautiously approving); Thomas C. Grey, "*Bowers v. Hardwick* Diminished," 68 *U. Colo. L. Rev.* 373 (1997) (approving).

d. Daniel Farber & Suzanna Sherry, "The Pariah Principle", 13 *Const. Comm.* 257 (1996), as well as Akhil Amar, "Attainder and Amendment 2: *Romer's* Rightness," 95 *Mich. L. Rev.* 203 (1996).

pervasive discrimination against a vulnerable group similar to those the state does protect;[e]

(e) the law's goal—state action reflecting widespread animus against gay people—was impermissible;[f]

(f) the measure, unprecedented in its sweep, was excessively overbroad.[g]

Which basis is the *best* basis for *Evans*? By *best*, one might mean the reason that is most consistent with (1) what the Court said in *Evans*, or (2) the Court's sex-and-gender equality jurisprudence generally, or (3) the normative theory of equality that the Court should be following in the sex, gender, and sexual orientation cases.

2. *Reality Check: The Amendment 2 Ballot Materials.* In Chapter 8, § 2C of this Supplement (pp. 93–100), we have reprinted, with the gracious permission of Colorado For Coalition for Family Values, the primary ballot materials developed by the sponsors of Amendment 2. You might want to read these materials at this point, as they might help you evaluate the Kennedy–Scalia debate: Is Amendment 2 properly viewed as reflecting antigay *animus* (Kennedy), or is it an expression of *public values* by tolerant Coloradans (Scalia)?

3. *Consequences of the Court's Decision in* Evans. Under the *best theory* for *Evans* (note 1), how would you evaluate the constitutionality of (a) the exclusion of gay people from the armed forces (Chapter 4, § 3 of the casebook), (b) state laws criminalizing only homosexual, but not heterosexual sodomy (casebook, pp. 38–39 nn."d" and "f"), and (c) state rules against adoption, foster parenting, or child custody by openly lesbian, bisexual, or gay parents (Chapter 9, § 3 of the casebook)? If Justice Scalia is correct that *Evans* and *Hardwick* are inconsistent, should *Hardwick* now be overruled?

The next several cases in this Supplement press the doctrinal consequences of *Evans* for other antigay ballot initiatives (*Equality Foundation*,

---

e. Louis Michael Seidman, "*Romer's* Radicalism: The Unexpected Revival of Warren Court Activism," 1996 *Sup. Ct. Rev.* 67; Jane Schachter, "*Romer v. Evans* and Democracy's Domain," 50 *Vand. L. Rev.* 361 (1997).

f. Andrew M. Jacobs, "*Romer* Wasn't Built in a Day: The Subtle Transformation in Judicial Argument over Gay Rights," 1996 *Wis. L. Rev.* 893; Andrew Koppelman, "*Romer v. Evans* and Invidious Intent," 6 *Wm. & Mary Bill of Rights J.* 89 (1997); Cass Sunstein, "The Supreme Court, 1995 Term—Foreword: Leaving Things Undecided," 110 *Harv. L. Rev.* 4, 62 (1996).

g. Richard Duncan, "The Narrow and Shallow Bite of *Romer* and the Eminent Rationality of Dual–Gender Marriage: A (Partial) Response to Professor Koppelman," 6 *Wm. & Mary Bill of Rights J.* 147 (1997). See also Janet E. Halley, "*Romer* v. *Hardwick*," 68 *U. Colo. L. Rev.* 429 (1997), who argues that the outcome hinges not only on the breadth of the harm caused by Amendment 2, but also on its potential for an endless accretion of everyday, minute, micro acts of discrimination that could never be prevented because of the bar against civil rights protections.

the next case), selective police action targeted at lesbians or gay men (*Stemler*, the case after *Equality Foundation*), and the legality of policies barring open lesbians, gay men, or bisexuals from certain public employment (*Shahar*, the final case in this chapter).

Equality Foundation of Greater Cincinnati, et al. v. City of Cincinnati, et al.

United States Court of Appeals for the Sixth Circuit, 1997.
128 F.3d 289, *rehearing en banc denied*, 1998 WL 101701 (1998).

■ CIRCUIT JUDGE KRUPANSKY.

[At issue was the constitutionality of an amendment to the City Charter of Cincinnati ("the Cincinnati Charter Amendment" or "Article XII"), adapted by popular vote, which read:

> NO SPECIAL CLASS STATUS MAY BE GRANTED BASED UPON SEXUAL ORIENTATION, CONDUCT OR RELATIONSHIPS.
>
> The City of Cincinnati and its various Boards and Commissions may not enact, adopt, enforce or administer any ordinance, regulation, rule or policy which provides that homosexual, lesbian, or bisexual orientation, status, conduct, or relationship constitutes, entitles, or otherwise provides a person with the basis to have any claim of minority or protected status, quota preference or other preferential treatment. This provision of the City Charter shall in all respects be self-executing. Any ordinance, regulation, rule or policy enacted before this amendment is adopted that violates the foregoing prohibition shall be null and void and of no force or effect. * * *

A panel of the Sixth Circuit initially upheld the Amendment. *Equality Foundation I*, 54 F.3d 261 (6th Cir.1995). Subsequent to that decision, in *Romer v. Evans*, the Supreme Court invalidated Colorado Amendment 2. (See text of Amendment 2 on p. 94 of casebook.). The Court directed the Sixth Circuit to reconsider its previous ruling in light of *Romer v. Evans*.]

* * * [T]he language of the Cincinnati Charter Amendment, read in its full context, merely prevented homosexuals, as homosexuals, from obtaining special privileges and preferences (such as affirmative action preferences or the legally sanctioned power to force employers, landlords, and merchants to transact business with them) from the City. In stark contrast, Colorado Amendment 2's far broader language could be construed to exclude homosexuals from the protection of every Colorado state law, including laws generally applicable to all other Coloradans, thus rendering gay people without recourse to any state authority at any level of government for any type of victimization or abuse which they might suffer by either private or public actors. Whereas Colorado Amendment 2 ominously threatened to reduce an entire segment of the state's population to the status of virtual non-citizens (or even non-persons) without legal rights

under any and every type of state law, the Cincinnati Charter Amendment had no such sweeping and conscience-shocking effect, because (1) it applied only at the lowest (municipal) level of government and thus could not dispossess gay Cincinnatians of any rights derived from any higher level of state law and enforced by a superior apparatus of state government, and (2) its narrow, restrictive language could not be construed to deprive homosexuals of all legal protections even under municipal law, but instead eliminated only "special class status" and "preferential treatment" for gays as gays under Cincinnati ordinances and policies, leaving untouched the application, to gay citizens, of any and all legal rights generally accorded by the municipal government to all persons as persons.

At bottom, the Supreme Court in *Romer* found that a state constitutional proviso which deprived a politically unpopular minority, but no others, of the political ability to obtain special legislation at every level of state government, including within local jurisdictions having pro-gay rights majorities, with the only possible recourse available through surmounting the formidable political obstacle of securing a rescinding amendment to the state constitution, was simply so obviously and fundamentally inequitable, arbitrary, and oppressive that it literally violated basic equal protection values. Thus, the Supreme Court directed that the ordinary three-part equal protection query was rendered irrelevant. See *Romer*, 116 S. Ct. at 1627 (noting that Colorado Amendment 2 "defies" conventional equal protection analysis).

This "extra-conventional" application of equal protection principles can have no pertinence to the case *sub judice*. The low level of government at which Article XII becomes operative is significant because the opponents of that strictly local enactment need not undertake the monumental political task of procuring an amendment to the Ohio Constitution as a precondition to achievement of a desired change in the local law, but instead may either seek local repeal of the subject amendment through ordinary municipal political processes, or pursue relief from every higher level of Ohio government including but not limited to Hamilton County, state agencies, the Ohio legislature, or the voters themselves via a statewide initiative.

Moreover, unlike Colorado Amendment 2, which interfered with the expression of local community preferences in that state, the Cincinnati Charter Amendment constituted a direct expression of the local community will on a subject of direct consequences to the voters. Patently, a local measure adopted by direct franchise, designed in part to preserve community values and character, which does not impinge upon any fundamental right or the interests of any suspect or quasi-suspect class, carries a formidable presumption of legitimacy and is thus entitled to the highest degree of deference from the courts.

* * * In any event, *Romer* should not be construed to forbid local electorates the authority, via initiative, to instruct their elected city council

representatives, or their elected or appointed municipal officers, to withhold special rights, privileges, and protections from homosexuals, or to prospectively remove the authority of such public representatives and officers to accord special rights, privileges, and protections to any non-suspect and non-quasi-suspect group. Such a reading would disenfranchise the voters of their most fundamental right which is the very foundation of the democratic form of government, even through the lowest (and most populist) organs and avenues of state government, to vote to override or preempt any policy or practice implemented or contemplated by their subordinate civil servants to bestow special rights, protections, and/or privileges upon a group of people who do not comprise a suspect or a quasi-suspect class and hence are not constitutionally entitled to any special favorable legal status. * * *

Accordingly, the *Romer* majority's rejection of rational relationship assessment hinged upon the wide breadth of Colorado Amendment 2, which deprived a politically unpopular minority of the opportunity to secure special rights at every level of state law. The uniqueness of Colorado Amendment 2's sweeping scope and effect differentiated it from the "ordinary case" in which a law adversely affects a discernable group in a relatively discrete manner and limited degree. In this context, the Court found that the rationales proffered by the state in support of Colorado Amendment 2 could not be justified, because the scope and effect of Colorado Amendment 2 "raise the inevitable inference that the disadvantage imposed is born of animosity toward the class of persons affected." *Id.* at 1628. * * *

In contradistinction, as evolved herein, the Cincinnati Charter Amendment constituted local legislation of purely local scope. As such, the City's voters had clear, actual, and direct individual and collective interests in that measure, and in the potential cost savings and other contingent benefits which could result from that local law. Beyond contradiction, passage of the Cincinnati Charter Amendment was not facially animated solely by an impermissible naked desire of a majority of the City's residents to injure an unpopular group of citizens, rather than to legally actualize their individual and collective interests and preferences. Clearly, the Cincinnati Charter Amendment implicated at least one issue of direct, actual, and practical importance to those who voted it into law, namely whether those voters would be legally compelled by municipal ordinances to expend their own public and private resources to guarantee and enforce nondiscrimination against gays in local commercial transactions and social intercourse.

Unquestionably, the Cincinnati Charter Amendment's removal of homosexuals from the ranks of persons protected by municipal antidiscrimination ordinances, and its preclusion of restoring that group to protected status, would eliminate and forestall the substantial public costs that accrue from the investigation and adjudication of sexual orientation discrimination complaints, which costs the City alone would otherwise bear because no coextensive protection exists under federal or state law. Moreover, the elimination of actionable special rights extended by city ordinances, and prevention of the reinstatement of such ordinances, would effectively advance the legitimate governmental interest of reducing the exposure of the City's residents to protracted and costly litigation by eliminating a municipally-created class of legal claims and charges, thus necessarily saving the City and its citizens, including property owners and employers, the costs of defending against such actions. * * *

In summary, the Cincinnati Charter Amendment did not disempower a group of citizens from attaining special protection at all levels of state government, but instead merely removed municipally enacted special protection from gays and lesbians. Unlike Colorado Amendment 2, the Cincinnati Charter Amendment cannot be characterized as an irrational measure fashioned only to harm an unpopular segment of the population in a sweeping and unjustifiable manner. * * *

Quaere: Did the Sixth Circuit persuasively distinguish *Romer v. Evans*? As this Supplement goes to press in July 1998, a petition for *certiorari* is pending before the Supreme Court.

Susan Stemler v. City of Florence, et. al.

United States Court of Appeals for the Sixth Circuit, 1997.
126 F.3d 856.

■ CIRCUIT JUDGE BOGGS

[The case began when Steve Kritis and his girlfriend Conni Black began fighting while at a bar in Florence, Kentucky. Both had been drinking heavily. Kritis became violent, repeatedly hitting Black and screaming at her. Black asked Laura Stemler, whom she met in the restroom, to drive her home. This enraged Kritis, who chased Stemler's car, trying to drive it off the road. A witness who had seen the chase called the police, and an officer pulled the two vehicles over. Stemler ran to the police car and told the officer that Kritis had assaulted both her and Black, had threatened to kill her, and then had chased them at high speed. Meanwhile, other officers arrived, and one of them spoke to Kritis. Kritis told the officer that Stemler was a lesbian and that he did not want his girlfriend to be with her. This officer told the other officers at the scene that Stemler was a lesbian. One of them placed Stemler under arrest for drunken driving. Another approached Black and told her that she would be arrested for public intoxication unless she left with Kritis. Black was too drunk to respond, and two officers lifted her out of Stemler's car and placed her in Kritis's truck. Kritis then drove away; he was not arrested, despite what witnesses described as his obvious intoxication. A short time later, Kritis lost control of the truck and crashed into a guardrail. The impact killed Black. Stemler, who denied that she is lesbian, filed a lawsuit.]

* * * We believe that this is the rare case in which a plaintiff has successfully stated a claim of selective prosecution. Stemler's complaint adequately alleges, and the record evidence supports a finding, that the defendant officers chose to arrest and prosecute her for driving under the influence because they perceived her to be a lesbian, and out of a desire to effectuate an animus against homosexuals. Each of the defendants was aware of Kritis's assertion that Stemler was a lesbian, and [Officer] Dusing admitted that he relied on Kritis's version of the facts in deciding to arrest Stemler. Furthermore, the record supports a finding that Kritis was similarly situated to Stemler (or, indeed, far drunker than she), that the defendant officers perceived Kritis to be heterosexual, and that consequently they chose not to arrest him at the same time that they arrested Stemler.

The defendants concede that Stemler's complaint alleges, and the record evidence could support a finding, that they decided to arrest and prosecute her because they perceived her to be a lesbian. They do not attempt to assert any justification whatsoever for this decision; instead they argue that as a blanket matter it is always constitutional to discriminate on the basis of sexual orientation, citing *Bowers v. Hardwick*. However, *Bowers* held only that there is no substantive due process right to engage in homosexual sodomy, and expressly declined to consider an equal protection claim. It is inconceivable that *Bowers* stands for the proposition that the state may discriminate against individuals on the basis of their sexual orientation solely out of animus to that orientation.* * * Since governmental action "must bear a rational relationship to a legitimate governmental purpose," *Romer*, and the desire to effectuate one's animus against homosexuals can never be a legitimate governmental purpose, a state action based on that animus alone violates the Equal Protection Clause. * * *

It is beyond cavil that Stemler has adequately alleged a selective-enforcement claim here. The record supports a finding that she was perceived to be a member of "an identifiable group," and that defendants sought to implement their animus against that group by arresting and seeking to prosecute her. The defendant officers are unable, and indeed have not even attempted, to demonstrate that there is any conceivable rational basis for a decision to enforce the drunk-driving laws against homosexuals but not against heterosexuals. The defendants can rely only on their assertion that discrimination on the basis of sexual orientation should be accorded no scrutiny whatsoever. We emphatically reject this assertion; the proposition that the state may constitutionally discriminate by enforcing laws only against homosexuals (or Centre College graduates or SAE members) is not now, and never has been, the law. Under the facts as we are obligated to construe them, the defendants violated the core principle of the Equal Protection Clause by choosing to exercise the power of the state against Stemler solely for the reason that they disapproved of her perceived sexual orientation. Thus, the dismissal of her complaint must be reversed. * * *

■ CIRCUIT JUDGE WELLFORD, concurring.

* * * I cannot equate an alleged animus against Stemler because of a perception about her sexual proclivities with discrimination based upon race, sex, national origin, or the like. There may be enough basis in Stemler's claim that some individual defendants based their law enforcement actions on some arbitrary and capricious classification or selectively enforced the laws on drunken driving, public intoxication, or public endangerment to warrant our reversing the dismissal of this claim. However, I do not reach the categorical decision of Judge Boggs that disapproval of Stemler's perceived sexual orientation was the sole, or even a significant, basis for her arrest by the defendants, and that this action therefore violated the equal protection clause. * * *

PART C. INTIMATE ASSOCIATION

Page 124. Substitute the following for the panel decision in *Shahar v. Bowers* which appears in the text:

Robin Joy Shahar v. Michael Bowers

U.S. Court of Appeals for the Eleventh Circuit, 1997 (*en banc*).
114 F.3d 1097 (11th Cir.1997), *cert. denied*, 118 S.Ct. 693 (1998).

■ CIRCUIT JUDGE EDMONDSON:

In this government-employment case, Plaintiff–Appellant contends that the Attorney General of the State of Georgia violated her federal constitutional rights by revoking an employment offer because of her purported "marriage"[1] to another woman. The district court concluded that Plaintiff's rights had not been violated. We affirm.

Given the culture and traditions of the Nation, considerable doubt exists that Plaintiff has a constitutionally protected federal right to be "married" to another woman: the question about the right of intimate association. Given especially that Plaintiff's religion requires a woman neither to "marry" another female—even in the case of lesbian couples—nor to marry at all, considerable doubt also exists that she has a constitutionally protected federal right to be "married" to another woman to engage in her religion: the question about the right of expressive association. * * *

Because even a favorable decision on these constitutional questions would entitle Plaintiff to no relief in this case, powerful considerations of judicial restraint call upon us not to decide these constitutional issues.

---

1. For clarity's sake, we use the words "marriage" and "wedding" (in quotation marks) to refer to Shahar's relationship with her partner; we use the word marriage (absent quotation marks) to indicate legally recognized heterosexual marriage.

* * * So, today we do stop short of making a final decision about such claimed rights. Instead, we assume (for the sake of argument only) that Plaintiff has these rights; but we conclude that the Attorney General's act—as an employer—was still lawful. * * *

II

Even when we assume, for argument's sake, that either the right to intimate association or the right to expressive association or both are present, we know they are not absolute. * * * Georgia and its elected Attorney General also have rights and duties which must be taken into account, especially where (as here) the State is acting as employer. * * * We also know that because the government's role as employer is different from its role as sovereign, we review its acts differently in the different contexts. In reviewing Shahar's claim, we stress that this case is about the government acting as employer.

* * * We conclude that the appropriate test for evaluating the constitutional implications of the State of Georgia's decision—as an employer—to withdraw Shahar's job offer based on her "marriage" is the same test as the test for evaluating the constitutional implications of a government employer's decision based on an employee's exercise of her right to free speech, that is, the *Pickering* balancing test.

We have previously pointed out that government employees who have access to their employer's confidences or who act as spokespersons for their employers, as well as those employees with some policy-making role, are in a special class of employees and might seldom prevail under the First Amendment in keeping their jobs when they conflict with their employers. * * *

Put differently, the government employer's interest in staffing its offices with persons the employer fully trusts is given great weight when the pertinent employee helps make policy, handles confidential information or must speak or act—for others to see—on the employer's behalf. Staff Attorneys inherently do (or must be ready to do) important things, which require the capacity to exercise good sense and discretion (as the Attorney General, using his considered judgment, defines those qualities): advise about policy; have access to confidential information (for example, litigation strategies); speak, write and act on behalf of the Attorney General and for the State.

In a case such as this one, the employee faces a difficult situation. In fact, we know of no federal appellate decision in which a subordinate prosecutor, state's attorney or like lawyer has prevailed in keeping his job over the chief lawyer's objection. We conclude that the Attorney General— who is an elected official with great duties and with no job security except that which might come from his office's performing well—may properly limit the lawyers on his professional staff to persons in whom he has trust.

As both parties acknowledge, this case arises against the backdrop of an ongoing controversy in Georgia about homosexual sodomy, homosexual marriages, and other related issues, including a sodomy prosecution—in which the Attorney General's staff was engaged—resulting in the well-known Supreme Court decision in *Bowers v. Hardwick*. When the Attorney General viewed Shahar's decision to "wed" openly—complete with changing her name—another woman (in a large "wedding") against this background of ongoing controversy, he saw her acts as having a realistic likelihood to affect her (and, therefore, the Department's) credibility, to interfere with the Department's ability to handle certain kinds of controversial matters (such as claims to same-sex marriage licenses, homosexual parental rights, employee benefits, insurance coverage of "domestic partners"), to interfere with the Department's efforts to enforce Georgia's laws against homosexual sodomy, and to create other difficulties within the Department which would be likely to harm the public perception of the Department.

In addition, because of Shahar's decision to participate in such a controversial same-sex "wedding" and "marriage" and the fact that she seemingly did not appreciate the importance of appearances and the need to avoid bringing "controversy" to the Department, the Attorney General lost confidence in her ability to make good judgments for the Department.

Whatever our individual, personal estimates might be, we—as we observe throughout this opinion—cannot say that the Attorney General's worries and view of the circumstances that led him to take the adverse personnel action against Shahar are beyond the broad range of reasonable assessments of the facts.

* * * To decide this case, we are willing to accord Shahar's claimed associational rights (which we have assumed to exist) substantial weight. But, we know that the weight due intimate associational rights, such as those involved in even a state-authorized marriage, can be overcome by a government employer's interest in maintaining the effective functioning of his office.

In weighing her interest in her associational rights, Shahar asks us also to consider the "non-employment related context" of her "wedding" and "marriage" and that "[s]he took no action to transform her intimate association into a public or political statement." In addition, Shahar says that we should take into account that she has affirmatively disavowed a right to benefits from the Department based on her "marriage."

To the extent that Shahar disclaims benefits bestowed by the State based on marriage, she is merely acknowledging what is undisputed, that Georgia law does not and has not recognized homosexual marriage. * * * We fail to see how that technical acknowledgment counts for much in the balance.

If Shahar is arguing that she does not hold herself out as "married," the undisputed facts are to the contrary. Department employees, among many others, were invited to a "Jewish, lesbian-feminist, out-door wedding" which included exchanging wedding rings: the wearing of a wedding ring is an outward sign of having entered into marriage. Shahar listed her "marital status" on her employment application as "engaged" and indicated that her future spouse was a woman. She and her partner have both legally changed their family name to Shahar by filing a name change petition with the Fulton County Superior Court. They sought and received the married rate on their insurance. And, they, together, own the house in which they cohabit. These things were not done secretly, but openly.

Even if Shahar is not married to another woman, she, for appearance purposes, might as well be. We suppose that Shahar could have done more to "transform" her intimate relationship into a public statement. But after (as she says) "sanctifying" the relationship with a large "wedding" ceremony by which she became—and remains for all to see—"married," she has done enough to warrant the Attorney General's concern.[2] He could conclude that her acts would give rise to a likelihood of confusion in the minds of members of the public: confusion about her marital status and about his attitude on same-sex marriage and related issues.

As for disruption within the Department, Shahar argues that we may discount the potential harm based on (what she sees as) the weakness of the Attorney General's predictions. Shahar overstates the Attorney General's "evidentiary burden."

In *Connick v. Myers*, 461 U.S. 138 (1983), the Supreme Court upheld the termination of an assistant district attorney based on her exercise of her free speech rights. In so doing, the Court noted the close working relationship involved in a district attorney's office (which we think is similar to the Department) and held as follows:

> When close working relationships are essential to fulfilling public responsibilities, a wide degree of deference to the employer's judgment is appropriate. Furthermore, we do not see the necessity for an employer to allow events to unfold to the extent that the disruption of the office and the destruction of working relationships is manifest before taking action.

---

2. We recognize that some of these acts (the exchange of rings, the insurance and property ownership) may not have been known by the Attorney General when he decided to withdraw Shahar's job offer. We can still consider them. First, these additional facts do not change the reason—Shahar's "wedding" and "marriage"—for the withdrawal of the job offer. Second, in balancing the Attorney General's interests with Shahar's, the facts of Shahar's subsequent conduct are evidence of the reasonableness of the Attorney General's concerns (about potential public knowledge and perception) at the time he made his decision. By the way, Shahar has requested "reinstatement" as part of her "relief." "After-acquired evidence" can be especially relevant in that context. *McKennon v. Nashville Banner Publ. Co.*, 513 U.S. 352 (1995).

Id. at 150–52.

As we have already written, the Attorney General's worry about his office being involved in litigation in which Shahar's special personal interest might appear to be in conflict with the State's position has been borne out in fact. This worry is not unreasonable. In addition, the Department, when the job offer was withdrawn, had already engaged in and won a recent battle about homosexual sodomy—highly visible litigation in which its lawyers worked to uphold the lawful prohibition of homosexual sodomy. This history makes it particularly reasonable for the Attorney General to worry about the internal consequences for his professional staff (for example, loss of morale, loss of cohesiveness and so forth) of allowing a lawyer, who openly—for instance, on her employment application and in statements to coworkers—represents herself to be "married" to a person of the same sex, to become part of his staff. Doubt and uncertainty of purpose can undo an office; he is not unreasonable to guard against that potentiality.

Shahar also argues that, at the Department, she would have handled mostly death penalty appeals and that the *Pickering* test requires evidence of potential interference with these particular duties. Even assuming Shahar is correct about her likely assignment within the Department, a particularized showing of interference with the provision of public services is not required. * * * In addition, the Attorney General must be able to reassign his limited legal staff as the needs of his office require. * * *

As we have already touched upon, the Attorney General, for balancing purposes, has pointed out, among other things, his concern about the public's reaction—the public that elected him and that he serves—to his having a Staff Attorney who is part of a same-sex "marriage." Shahar argues that he may not justify his decision by reference to perceived public hostility to her "marriage." We have held otherwise about the significance of public perception when law enforcement is involved. In *McMullen v. Carson*, 754 F.2d 936 (11th Cir.1985), we held that a sheriff's clerical employee's First Amendment interest in an off-duty statement that he was employed by the sheriff's office and also was a recruiter for the Ku Klux Klan was outweighed by the sheriff's interest in esprit de corps and credibility in the community the sheriff policed. More important, we relied, in large part, on public perceptions of the employee's constitutionally protected act.

In *McMullen*, both public perception and the anticipated effect that the employee's constitutionally protected activity would have on cohesion within the office were crucial in tipping the scales in the sheriff's favor. Nothing indicates that the employee had engaged in a criminal act or that he had joined an organization (he had joined the Invisible Empire) that had engaged in any criminal act. Given that it was additionally undisputed that neither the employee's statements nor his protected expressive association hindered his ability to perform his clerical duties and that the specific clerk "performed his duties in exemplary fashion," *id.* at 937, the two factors—

public perception and anticipated effect—seemed to be the only ones weighing on the sheriff's side of the scale. But that was enough.

This case is different from *McMullen* in some ways, but *McMullen* guides us about the significance of "public perception." In this case, the Attorney General was similarly entitled to consider any "deleterious effect on [his] ability to enforce the law of the community," *id.*, and that "[u]nder our system of Government, that duty [law enforcement] can be performed only with the consent of the vast majority. . . . Efficient law enforcement requires mutual respect, trust and support." *Id.* at 939.

The Attorney General was also entitled to conclude that the public may think that employment of a Staff Attorney who openly purports to be part of a same-sex "marriage" is, at best, inconsistent with the other positions taken or likely to be taken by the Attorney General as the state's chief legal officer. The Attorney General has a right to take steps to protect the public from confusion about his stand and the Law Department's stand on controversial matters, such as same-sex marriage.

* * * Shahar says that by taking into account these concerns about public reaction, the Attorney General impermissibly discriminated against homosexuals; and she refers us to the Supreme Court's recent decision in *Romer v. Evans.*

* * * *Romer* is about people's condition; this case is about a person's conduct. And, *Romer* is no employment case. Considering (in deciding to revoke a job offer) public reaction to a future Staff Attorney's conduct in taking part in a same-sex "wedding" and subsequent "marriage" is not the same kind of decision as an across-the-board denial of legal protection to a group because of their condition, that is, sexual orientation or preference.

* * * We stress in this case the sensitive nature of the pertinent professional employment. And we hold that the Attorney General's interest—that is, the State of Georgia's interest—as an employer in promoting the efficiency of the Law Department's important public service does outweigh Shahar's personal associational interests.

We do not decide today that the Attorney General did or did not do the right thing when he withdrew the pertinent employment offer. That decision is properly not ours to make. What we decide is much different and less: For the Law Department's professional staff, Georgia's Attorney General has made a personnel decision which none of the asserted federal constitutional provisions prohibited him from making.

■ CIRCUIT JUDGE TJOFLAT, specially concurring:

* * * The court engages in *Pickering* balancing in an effort to avoid the question whether the Constitution protects the First and Fourteenth Amendment rights Shahar seeks to enforce. I agree that constitutional questions should be answered only when necessary to the resolution of the case. In this case, however, I believe the court must reach the constitutional question in order to determine under *Pickering* whether the Attorney

General's action was lawful. As I explain below, the court must describe qualitatively the constitutional right it is placing on the scale in order to determine whether, on balance, the government's interest is to prevail. The court does not do this—it does not tell us, with respect to each of Shahar's remaining claims, where the assumed right ranks in the constitutional hierarchy

* * * I submit that if one assumes that the First Amendment protects the homosexual relationship between Shahar and her partner as an intimate association, summary judgment on the intimate association claim was inappropriate on the record before us. Thus, I reach the question whether that relationship has First Amendment protection. I conclude that it does not. As for Shahar's claims that the Attorney General based his employment decision on Shahar's participation in the religious wedding ceremony and thus infringed her rights of free exercise of religion and expressive association, I conclude that the claims fail for want of proof that the religious nature of that ceremony motivated, in whole or in part, the Attorney General's decision. I turn first to Shahar's intimate association claim.

Shahar argues that the Attorney General's withdrawal of the offer of employment violated her right to intimate association with her partner. The Supreme Court articulated the right to intimate association in *Roberts v. United States Jaycees*, 468 U.S. 609 (1984). * * * The Court in *Roberts* provided some guidance in determining which relationships are entitled to protection as intimate associations. Roberts provides a list of "factors that may be relevant [to determining whether a given relationship constitutes an intimate association], includ[ing] size, purpose, policies, selectivity, congeniality, and other characteristics that in a particular case may be pertinent." 468 U.S. at 620. While these factors may be relevant, I believe that courts must also determine whether the asserted relationship has "played a critical role in the culture and traditions of the Nation by cultivating and transmitting shared ideals and beliefs." *Id.* at 618–19.

In its most recent case to address the issue of intimate association, *FW/PBS, Inc. v. City of Dallas*, 493 U.S. 215 (1990), the Court [upheld] a municipal ordinance that required a license for any motel renting rooms for fewer than ten hours [against a claim that it infringed] a hotel patron's intimate association rights. This [decision] illustrates the Court's view that "the culture and traditions of the Nation" are critical to the determination of whether a particular relationship is entitled to protection as an intimate association. * * * [I]n order to find that Shahar's relationship is protected as an intimate association, we must find that homosexual relationships have "played a critical role in the culture and traditions of the Nation by cultivating and transmitting shared ideals and beliefs."

I conclude that this simply is not the case. Shahar has pointed to nothing to suggest that homosexual relationships have played a critical role in our history and tradition. On the contrary, the Supreme Court's decision in *Bowers v. Hardwick*, suggests that homosexual relationships have not played such a role. In that case the Court concluded that there is no fundamental right to engage in homosexual sodomy. In arriving at that conclusion, the Court stated that "[n]o connection between family, marriage, or procreation on the one hand and homosexual activity on the other has been demonstrated." *Id.* at 191. The Court concluded that "to claim that a right to engage in [homosexual sodomy] is deeply rooted in this Nation's history and tradition or implicit in the concept of ordered liberty is, at best, facetious." *Id.* at 194.

Homosexual relationships have not played the same role as marital or familial relationships in the history and traditions of the Nation. Shahar's relationship with her partner is not a "fundamental element of personal liberty" protected as an intimate association. As a result, Shahar fails to state a claim that her right to intimate association has been violated. Summary judgment on this claim was therefore appropriate.

* * * If Shahar's relationship is entitled to the same level of protection as is a heterosexual marriage, I doubt whether the public perception of that relationship, or the State of Georgia's public policy against according such relationships the same protections and privileges as heterosexual marriage, would be placed on the government's side of the scale. Even if those factors were weighed in the balance, it is difficult to imagine that they would outweigh Shahar's interest in her relationship.

A hypothetical will illustrate the point. Suppose that Shahar had married a man of another race rather than "marrying" a woman. Such a relationship would clearly be protected as an intimate association. I believe that a court engaged in a *Pickering* balance would either (1) refuse to consider as government interests the public perception of such a relationship or any state policy positions hostile toward that relationship, or (2) conclude that such governmental interests do not prevail in the balance. In short, if the court accords Shahar's relationship the same constitutional value that the Supreme Court has assigned to heterosexual marriage, the Attorney General would face a heavy burden in prevailing in a *Pickering* balance.

* * * I fail to see how the court can avoid the constitutional question whether Shahar's relationship with her partner is protected under the First and Fourteenth Amendments. For this reason, I cannot ascribe to the court's analysis of her intimate association claim. * * *

■ SENIOR CIRCUIT JUDGE GODBOLD dissenting, joined by JUDGES BARKETT and KRAVITCH:

* * * The intimate association Shahar asserts is not based upon false or sham assertions of religious belief, or hasty decision, or overnight conversion. She and her partner grew up in traditional Jewish families. Shahar attended Hebrew school from the third grade. She was bat mitzvahed at age 13 and continued in Hebrew school until she was confirmed at

age 16. Greenfield grew up in a conservative, kosher, Jewish home. She went through Jewish training through high school, attended Jewish summer camps, and was involved in Jewish youth groups.

Shahar and Greenfield have been significant participants in the life of their synagogue, located in Atlanta. It is affiliated with the Reconstructionist Movement, one of several movements within Judaism. The synagogue serves gays, lesbians, and heterosexuals. The Reconstructionist Movement is regarded as liberal in some respects but is conservative in others. Shahar has led services at the synagogue and has given several sermons. She and Greenfield often attend together. The proposed ceremony was announced at a service of the synagogue.

Their rabbi, Sharon Kleinbaum, counseled them in eight or nine formal premarital sessions and many informal ones. Rabbi Kleinbaum described the manner in which she satisfied herself of their commitment to the Jewish faith. She discussed with them "the seriousness of their commitment to the Jewish issues as well as to each other, and anything related to wedding ceremonies in general that, as a Rabbi, I would do." Continuing, she said, "I discussed with them the nature of their home life and the significance of Jewish practices to them and how it was inconceivable to them to do any kind of ceremony that was not a Jewish one." Rabbi Kleinbaum considers that the union in which they joined is a public affirmation of their commitment to each other and to the Jewish people, having no legal significance but only personal and religious significance, and that it can be terminated only by the church.

The evidence demonstrates without dispute that same-sex marriage is accepted within the Reconstructionist Movement of Judaism, that Shahar and her partner are committed to that belief, and that, in keeping with their Jewish principles, they carefully and thoughtfully prepared for marriage.

The evidence discloses that Judaism in the United States does not have a monolithic view of same-sex marriages. The Reconstructionist Movement accepts the concept of same-sex marriage, and many rabbis within the Movement perform such marriages. The Reconstructionists are working on a manual that will help guide rabbis performing same-sex marriages. Other movements in Judaism reject same-sex marriages, and still other movements are divided in view, with some rabbis performing such marriages and others declining to do so. But the critical facts are that Shahar and her partner are lifelong adherents to Judaism and good-faith, dedicated participants in the Reconstructionist Movement; the Reconstructionist Movement is a significant movement within American Judaism; and it regards same-sex marriages as acceptable and desirable in preference to couples living together without marriage.

The actual ceremony between Shahar and Greenfield occurred after the Attorney General terminated the agreement with her, but it is relevant to the fact that her association has religious basis and status. It was the culmination of a weekend of religious-centered activities that began Friday evening with a celebration of the Hebrew Sabbath, which extends from Friday evening to Saturday evening. The wedding occurred on Sunday. Essentially the ceremony followed the traditional ceremony for a heterosexual Jewish couple except for deletion of terms "bride" and "groom." It took place beneath the traditional canopy. The couple signed the traditional Kutubah, or written marriage contract. They exchanged rings in traditional fashion, and the traditional glass was broken. The traditional seven blessings were given, done in Hebrew and in English. Rabbi Kleinbaum was dressed in traditional garb. She described the event as a "Jewish religious ceremony," as a "Jewish marriage," and as a "Jewish wedding."

In her testimony Rabbi Kleinbaum explained the importance of the family to the survival of the Jewish people and the significance of the Jewish marriage ceremony to the creation of the family unit. Therefore, as she explained, the commitments made by Shahar and her partner through the marriage ceremony were not only commitments to each other but to their congregation and to all of the Jewish people as well.

* * * The termination letter is plainly based on the Attorney General's conclusion that Shahar was falsely holding herself out as becoming married in the civil and legal sense, i.e., proposing to engage in a "purported marriage." In search of evidence of holding out by Shahar this court relies upon her use of the words "marriage" and "wedding." This implicates differing perceptions of what words mean. In a common law/statutory/traditional sense "marriage" describes a ceremony as a relationship or status between two persons as defined by common law or statute, involving two heterosexual persons, one male and one female. But, as this case tells us, that is not the only and ineluctable meaning. To a person of Shahar's faith as a Reconstructionist Jew "marriage" refers to the formal Jewish wedding ceremony recommended and carried out pursuant to the participants' Jewish faith by two persons (including two homosexuals) who have made a lifelong commitment to each other and are bound to each other by the ceremony in a relationship that can be terminated only within their faith and who, by engaging in the ceremony, made a commitment to the Jewish people as well. "Marriage" also refers to the status thereby conveyed upon them. In the eyes of Shahar and her partner they engaged in a Jewish marriage and they are accepted by their faith as married and accordingly they may use the term "marriage" to refer to the ceremonial event and to the status created by it.

This court, in its footnote 1, recognizes the duality of meaning that I have described for "wedding" and "marriage" [and "spouse"]. Throughout its opinion the court attempts to indicate (not always successfully) by quotation marks and limiting words which meaning it is referring to. But the decision of the en banc court is based upon, and approves, the Attorney General's attribution to these words of only a single meaning, the statutory/common-law/traditional meaning, and his perception that any other meaning is either false or non-existent, i.e., Shahar proposed to engage in a "purported marriage." The court simply adopts one perception and excludes the other as though it did not exist for Shahar and for others of her faith.

What the Attorney General knew was that Shahar had used the terms "marriage" and "spouse" and "marriage ceremony" in referring to the ceremony she planned and to the status to be created by it. She had used the terms "honeymoon" or "wedding trip" in describing her plans. Within the office there was information that she planned to send, or had sent, invitations to the ceremony and that some staff members were on the invitation list, and other information that, as the Attorney General described it, the planned ceremony would be "a big or church wedding, I don't remember which." Possessed of some, or all, of this knowledge, the Attorney General neither saw Shahar nor talked to her but built a Chinese wall around himself and concluded that she had falsely invoked the civil/statutory/common-law meaning that he attributed to the terms. We know that it occurred to him that assigning a single meaning to "marriage" and "wedding ceremony" might not be correct, for he talked with a female Jewish member of his staff, who told him that the wedding was to be performed by a rabbi from New York who performed homosexual marriages but that "she was not aware of homosexual marriages or gay and lesbian marriages being recognized in Judaism." At best the response was ambiguous—on the one hand the wedding was to be done by a rabbi, but on the other hand the staff member was not aware that it would be recognized in Judaism. As it turned out, she was correct about the rabbi but incorrect or uninformed about recognition of the marriage.

Since the Attorney General neither saw nor talked with Shahar the decision by this court relies upon information supplied to him by senior staffers who had talked with him. The Attorney General was out of town when the matter first came up. Senior staffers met together several times and discussed their concerns and possible action. The group considered, but rejected, a suggestion that there be a meeting with Shahar to discuss the matter. After the Attorney General returned he met with staffers. He reached the conclusion that the job offer should be withdrawn. In a meeting with staffers the structure of a "termination meeting" with Shahar was worked out. The Attorney General would not be present at the meeting. A designated staffer (accompanied by a witness) was to meet with Shahar, tell her that the offer to her was withdrawn, and deliver to her the termination letter (in sealed form). The messenger was instructed to make no additional comments and to tell Shahar if she had comments they should be addressed to the Attorney General in writing. The staff member-spokesman prepared a written script of what he would say. Ironically, it concluded: "Thanks again for coming in and have a nice day." The scenario was played out. Shahar asked to see the Attorney General and was told that he was unavailable.

The Attorney General and his staff acted in ignorance of the religious roots of the association that Shahar planned, the centrality of it to her faith, and the recognition of it by the religion to which she was committed. Staff members could recall no discussion of or inquiry into the religious aspects of the matter. The actions by the Attorney General do not meet the constitutional requirements of reasonableness.

If the Attorney General had made reasonable investigation this case might never have arisen. But not only did he make no further investigation, he closed the door to knowledge. It would have been easy to confer with Shahar, or have an assistant do so, and explore her desire to use the term "marriage" and his concern about this usage. If she had then explained that she used the term as recommended and accepted by her faith, the Attorney General, correctly enlightened, might have been satisfied. On the other hand, he might have rejected her explanation as insufficient to ameliorate his concerns. He might have explained to her his fear of possible impact on his office and could have explored with her ways in which she might disseminate knowledge of the religious nature of her intimate association. What we do know is that neither the Attorney General, nor the staff members on whom this court implies that he relied, made inquiry into the religious nature of her plans beyond the ambiguous or mistaken response from the single Jewish staff member of whom the Attorney General inquired. The Attorney General walled himself off, forbade comment or inquiry by staff members who met with Shahar, and terminated the agreement with Shahar on his erroneous perception of the association that she was asserting. Whatever his views about possible adverse effects on his office, he did not act reasonably. * * *

■ SENIOR CIRCUIT JUDGE KRAVITCH dissenting, joined by JUDGES BARKETT and GODBOLD:

[Judge Kravitch agreed that *Pickering* involves a balancing test rather than a strict scrutiny standard.] * * * In my view, however, the *en banc* majority has employed a balancing test in name only. The *en banc* majority's opinion devotes paragraph after paragraph to Bowers' interests, but gives short shrift to Shahar's intimate associational interests. In contrast, Judge Godbold's dissenting opinion eloquently relates the sincerity and depth of feeling which underlies Shahar's connection to her partner. Because the association in question falls close to the familial end of the continuum of human relationships, I conclude that Shahar's interests weigh heavily in the *Pickering* balance.

On the other side of the balance, the *en banc* majority first considers Bowers' interests in the internal workings of his office. Bowers has not asserted that Shahar's association caused any actual disruption of the functioning of his staff. Instead, Bowers has forecast that Shahar's presence will undermine morale and create divisions within the Georgia Department of Law because some employees will view her association as a political statement inconsistent with state laws that the Department must enforce. The *en banc* majority correctly notes that courts must give "substantial weight to government employers' reasonable predictions of disruption...." *Waters v. Churchill*, 511 U.S. 661, 673. The Supreme Court, however, has rejected the notion that courts must accept blindly all claims of harm conjured by government employers. * * *

To the extent Bowers concluded Shahar would disrupt the office because her relationship could be interpreted as a political statement, he did not act reasonably. Shahar's association with her partner, although not secret, was private. Shahar's religious marriage ceremony was by invitation and was held in another state. It was neither announced in the newspapers, nor otherwise reported publicly. Further, Shahar never claimed she had contracted a legal marriage, nor did she challenge her legal ineligibility for civil marriage. Bowers could and should have ascertained all of these facts before he took action against Shahar. Instead, as Judge Godbold notes in his dissent, Bowers categorically refused to discuss his purported concerns with Shahar. Finally, the record confirms that Bowers had no factual basis to believe Shahar had violated the law or advocated violations of law. Because Bowers failed to act reasonably, his predictions regarding intra-office strife do not weigh very heavily in the balance.

Bowers' other main justification for his action centers around his fear of negative public reaction to his hiring of Shahar. Although public confidence certainly is a relevant concern for Bowers, it is important to note that catering to private prejudice is not a legitimate government interest. The *en banc* majority attempts to justify its emphasis on anticipated public hostility by pointing to *McMullen v. Carson*, 754 F.2d 936 (11th Cir.1985), a case in which this court considered public reaction to the presence of a Ku Klux Klan recruiter in a sheriff's office in affirming a governmental employment decision. *McMullen*, however, bears no relationship to this case.

First, unlike *McMullen*, where the employee publicized his association with the Klan on a television news broadcast, in this case, Shahar did not make any public statements. Further, the sheriff's decision in *McMullen* was not simply based on his prediction that the public would be biased against the Klan-affiliated employee. Rather, the record established that "*violent* racism has become the Klan's trademark ... [that] [d]ivisive, confrontational tactics are used by the Klan during periods of racial unrest in order to promote recruitment [and that] [t]hose tactics are still being used in Florida." *McMullen*, 754 F.2d at 938 (emphasis added). The sheriff and the community thus reasonably could conclude that the Klan recruiter sanctioned such inflammatory, often illegal, activities. In contrast, Bowers simply baldly asserted that public reaction to Shahar's pending employment with his office would have prevented him from serving the state effectively. In light of the Klan's undisputed history of criminal violence, public reaction in *McMullen* was not only more certain, but also likely would have been more severe than anything which reasonably might have been projected in this case. Finally, although public concern over the Klan's criminally violent activities is a legitimate basis for governmental action, the Supreme Court has now held that animosity toward gay people is an illegitimate purpose for state policy, and thus, to prevail in the balancing of interests, Bowers must cite more than perceived, public distaste for homosexuals. See generally *Romer v. Evans*.

The foregoing analysis leads me to conclude that, on the record of this case, Shahar's constitutional interest in pursuing her intimate association with her partner outweighs any threat to the operation of the Georgia Department of Law. * * *.

■ CIRCUIT JUDGE BIRCH dissenting, joined by JUDGES BARKETT, GODBOLD and KRAVITCH:

* * * I might have found the majority's application of the *Pickering* balancing test more convincing were it not for the Supreme Court's recent decision in *Romer v. Evans*. In my opinion, the Court's recognition in *Romer* that homosexuals, as a class, are entitled to some protection under the Equal Protection Clause bears on the validity—and therefore the weight in applying the *Pickering* balancing test—of Bowers' justifications for his action. With *Romer* in the balance, the scales tip decidedly in favor of Shahar because Bowers' asserted interests are not a legitimate basis for infringing Shahar's constitutionally-protected right of intimate association. * * *

The *Pickering* balance in this case requires us to measure Shahar's right of intimate association against Bowers' asserted interests in infringing that right in the context of an employment relationship. The weight we accord to Bowers' asserted interests, however, hinges entirely on the reasonableness of his predictions as to how Shahar's homosexual relationship might affect or disrupt the Attorney General's office; significantly, it is undisputed that Bowers has made no showing of actual disruption to the office. When we closely examine these predictions, we discover that each one is based on a series of assumptions and unsupported inferences about Shahar because of her status as a homosexual.[2] * * *

The first inference that Bowers drew from Shahar's status as a lesbian who married another woman is that the public might be hostile to her participation in a same-sex marriage and might view Shahar's employment

---

2. The distinction that the majority draws between Shahar's status as a homosexual and her conduct in entering into a homosexual marriage, is truly a distinction without a difference, in my opinion. It is a matter of simple logic that only homosexuals would enter into a homosexual marriage. Bowers' action, therefore, draws a distinction that, on its face, reaches homosexuals only and distinguishes among similarly situated people on the basis of one trait only: that they are homosexual. Bowers cannot escape this conclusion by subdividing the class of homosexuals into those who elect to enter into a homosexual marriage and those who do not, and then claiming that he discriminated against Shahar not because of her status as a homosexual, but because she is a homosexual and she entered into a homosexual marriage. * * *

by his Department as inconsistent with Georgia law. Bowers argued in his brief that "the public perception is that 'the natural consequence of a marriage is some sort of sexual conduct, . . . and if it's homosexual, it would have to be sodomy.' "As the Supreme Court made clear in *Palmore v. Sidoti*, 466 U.S. 429 (1984) [casebook, p. 831], the government may not transform private biases into legitimate state interests by relying on the prejudices of the public. * * *

In applying the principle of *Palmore* to this case, the key question is not whether the government official reasonably could assume that the public might have a negative reaction to the employee's presence; it is whether the public's perception upon which the official relies is itself a legitimate basis for government action. If the public's perception is borne of no more than unsupported assumptions and stereotypes, it is irrational and cannot serve as the basis of legitimate government action. In this instance, the public's (alleged) blanket assumption that "if it's homosexual, it would have to be sodomy" is based not on anything set forth in the record but rather on public stereotyping and animosity toward homosexuals. Under the principles articulated in *Romer*, this does not provide the state with a legitimate, rational basis to discriminate against Shahar. Bowers' "concern" for the public's perception of homosexuals, therefore, is entitled to no weight in balancing Shahar's right of intimate association.

* * * Bowers' argument with respect to the alleged deleterious effect of Shahar's status and conduct on "morale" within the office is another attempt to legitimize his adverse action against Shahar on the basis of inferences that others—here, his employees—might derive from her status as a lesbian. The inferences from Shahar's acknowledged homosexuality that she is likely to violate Georgia's sodomy law, or would be unable or unwilling to enforce Georgia's sodomy or marriage laws, is no more justified on behalf of Bowers or his employees than it is on behalf of the public. Moreover, it is important to note that Bowers' speculation regarding Shahar's ability to handle certain types of cases is just that: speculation. Bowers has emphatically refused to meet with Shahar to discuss any of his concerns. Compounding this deficiency in Bowers' assertion that his prediction is "reasonable" is the fact that Bowers does not make the same assumption with respect to any of his other employees: He does not assume, for instance, that an unmarried employee who is openly dating an individual of the opposite sex has likely committed fornication, a criminal offense in Georgia, and thus may have a potential conflict in enforcing the fornication law. Nor, for that matter, does he apparently assume that married employees could well have committed sodomy and could themselves have a potential conflict in enforcing Georgia's sodomy law.

In short, Bowers' asserted interests in taking adverse action against Shahar are based on inferences from her status as a homosexual which Bowers claims that he, the public, and department staff are entitled to make. In light of the Supreme Court's decision in *Romer*, these status-based inferences, unsupported by any facts in the record and explained only by animosity toward and stereotyping of homosexuals, do not constitute a legitimate interest that outweighs Shahar's First Amendment right of intimate association.* * *

[JUDGE BARKETT's dissenting opinion is omitted.]

NOTES ON THE *EN BANC* DECISION IN *SHAHAR*

1. *Weight of the Intimate Association Claim.* The majority's opinion stresses the discretion of a public employer, especially of a law enforcement official, to limit employees to those whom he or she "fully trusts" and about whom there is no negative public perception. The majority notes at the outset that this consideration is conclusive, regardless of whether Shahar's right of intimate association is valid. Judge Tjoflat agrees that *this* employment decision was lawful, but would not uphold the same act had the relationship been, for example, an interracial marriage. Under the majority's reasoning the nature of the relationship is the source of the problems of distrust and public disapproval. However, it is those same facts about the history of this relationship that the Godbold dissent and the Kravitch dissent rely on as indicia of why the balancing scales under *Pickering* tilt in Shahar's favor. How should a court resolve this deadlock? What kinds of objective criteria for assessing the comparative weights of the competing interests does Judge Kravitch suggest? Can you think of others?

2. *Private Bias or Public Credibility?* Judge Birch views the defendant's arguments as "status-based inferences * * * explained only by animosity toward and stereotyping of homosexuals." Is he correct to argue that *Romer v. Evans* (casebook, p. 93) compels the dismissal of defendant's concerns? Does it matter that the defendant is not only a public official but an elected one? That the dissenters cannot come up with a case where an appellate court has second-guessed personnel decisions of a state's attorney office, and that the leading Supreme Court decision counseling strong deference (*Connick*) arose in just such a setting? The different readings of the impact of *Romer v. Evans* that are evident in the majority opinion and the Birch dissent likely foreshadow the debate that will arise in the lower federal courts as they interpret that decision in the years to come. Compare Marjorie Rowland's case in Chapter 3 (casebook, pp. 301–04).

3. *The Meanings of Marriage.* One of the undertones of the majority decision is the implication not only that Shahar's relationship is something less than a real marriage (hence the quotation marks), but also that her actions in having such a ceremony provide evidence of the likelihood of loss of public confidence in the office of the attorney general. Compare this case to *Singer v. U.S. Civil Service Commission* [casebook, p. 892 of text]. Is *Shahar* another example of penalizing the "flaunting" of one's sexuality? Would a nexus test approach be useful to an intimate association claim?

SHAHAR POSTSCRIPT

In the week after the *en banc* decision was handed down, Attorney General Bowers announced that he had carried on an adulterous affair for more than a decade with a woman who previously worked in his office. Bowers had recently resigned as Attorney General and announced his candidacy for the Republican nomination for Governor of Georgia. Adultery is a crime in Georgia. News reports quoted Bowers as saying that "living in a situation of immorality while enforcing the law against somebody * * * [is] hypocritical morally," but that he had no second thoughts about his decisions to defend the state's sodomy law and to fire Shahar. Kevin Sack, "Georgia Candidate for Governor Admits Adultery and Resigns Commission in Guard," *N. Y. Times*, June 6, 1997, p. A29. Should this admission alter the legal considerations of the case? Meanwhile, Robin Shahar is employed as an assistant city attorney for the City of Atlanta.

CHAPTER 2

MEDICALIZATION OF SEX, GENDER AND SEXUALITY

SECTION 2

MEDICALIZATION AND AMERICAN LAW

PART B(3). CASE STUDY: THE PSYCHOPATHIC PERSONALITY EXCLUSION IN U.S. IMMIGRATION LAW

Page 189—We have rewritten the Postscript and have added a recent immigration decision to provide an international contrast:

POSTSCRIPTS: IMMIGRATION EXCLUSION OF HIV–INFECTED PEOPLE AND ASYLUM FOR GAY AND HIV–INFECTED PEOPLE

Just as the exclusion of gay people was being eliminated, a new exclusion was inserted. Senator Jesse Helms in 1987 sponsored an appropriations rider that directed the Department of Health and Human Services (HHS) to list AIDS (later, "HIV infection") as one of the infectious diseases for which noncitizens could be excluded from entering the United States. See Supplemental Appropriations Act, 1987, Pub. Law No. 100–71, § 518, 101 Stat. 475. The 1990 Act, which repealed the psychopathic personality and sexual deviation exclusion, also appeared to reverse the Helms Amendment, for it gave HHS discretion to determine "communicable diseases of a public health significance" which would trigger the new shorter list of immigration exclusions. 8 U.S.C. § 1182(a)(1)(A)(1).

In early 1993, HHS Secretary Donna Shalala announced her intention to remove HIV infection from the list of "communicable diseases" requiring exclusion. Congress responded with the NIH Revitalization Act of 1993, Pub. Law No. 103–43, § 2007, 107 Stat. 210, which amends the immigration statute, 8 U.S.C. § 1182(a)(1)(A)(i), to exclude HIV-infected people from entering the country. The HIV-infection ban remains in effect (as of 1998). To the extent HIV infection is associated with gay and bisexual men, the HIV infection exclusion becomes a partial replacement for the gay exclusion—a striking example of the medicalization of American anxieties about sexuality. Chapter 12, Section 1 contains a more thorough consideration of sexuality issues presented by HIV and AIDS.

As a postscript to the postscript, it is ironic, if not legally incoherent, that the INS has found that HIV-infected people can be refugees under federal immigration law which requires asylum to people who have a "well-founded fear of persecution on account of race, religion, nationality, membership in a particular social group, or political opinion." One INS adjudicator ruled that a West African man infected with HIV was entitled to asylum here because he showed that HIV-positive people in his country were denied medical care and socially mistreated. Dep't of Justice, Off. Imm. Rev., File A71 498 940 (1995). Less ironically, lesbians and gay men persecuted on the basis of their sexual orientation have for the entire decade been able to seek asylum in the United States. See *In re Tenorio* (1993) (Problem 8–6, casebook, pp. 760–61); this topic is treated in greater detail by a Note to Chapter 8, § 3C of this Supplement. Consider the following case which shows how medical attitudes once widely held by American doctors can now be the basis for asylum when still held by doctors in other countries.

Alla Konstantinova Pitcherskaia v. INS, 118 F.3d 641 (9th Cir.1997). Alla Konstantinova Pitcherskaia sought asylum from Russia in June 1992 on grounds of persecution for her anti-Communist political views; the INS Asylum Office found that she had in fact been persecuted for those views in the past but that, under the new non-Communist regime, she had no "well-founded fear" of future persecution and so denied her application. Pitcherskaia renewed her application on the additional ground that she had been and reasonably feared she would continue to be persecuted for her political activism on behalf of lesbians and gay men; she had not raised this ground originally, because she assertedly did not know that this was a basis for asylum.

The INS hearing officer found that Pitcherskaia had been arrested for her lesbian-rights activism on several occasions in the 1980s, her former girlfriend was sent to a psychiatric institution in 1985 or 1986 for electroshock and other treatment to "cure" her of her lesbian orientation and Pitcherskaia was herself listed as a "suspected lesbian" and required to undergo therapy sessions at the clinic, and in 1990–1991 she was detained and interrogated about her suspected sexual orientation. Since coming to the USA in 1992, Pitcherskaia has been presented with additional "Demands for Appearance" at a hospital to treat her for her lesbianism. She claims that lesbians in non-Communist Russia are still harassed and subjected to medical procedures such as electroshock.

The INS and then the Board of Immigration Appeals denied her application for asylum, on the ground that the Russian authorities' apparent intent was to "cure" her of what they considered a mental disease; hence, there was no "persecution" that is required for asylum. The Ninth Circuit, in an opinion by **Judge Fletcher**, reversed. The statutory term persecution must be read as " 'the infliction of suffering or harm upon those who differ ... in a way regarded as offensive.' " (Quoting *Sangha v. INS*, 103 F.3d 1482, 1487 [9th Cir. 1997].) Thus ostensibly "therapeutic" treatment can be persecution, if viewed from the eyes of the victim, and the Ninth Circuit remanded the case to the INS to determine whether Pitcherskaia met the other requirements for asylum.

PART C.   MEDICALIZATION, ABORTION AND THE CONTROL OF WOMEN'S SEXUALITY

Page 201—Add following Note 3:

4.   *Scope of the Best Interests Test.* If a young teenager (i.e. not a mature minor) is seeking to bypass a parental notification requirement, what exactly must she prove under the "best interests" test? The issue arose in Montana, where abortion rights advocates argued that the notice rule should be lifted if the minor could demonstrate that the abortion would be in her best interests, given all the circumstances. The Montana statute, however, specified that a minor had to prove that the notification requirement was contrary to her best interests. The Supreme Court upheld the statute and the more specific test in *Lambert v. Wicklund*, 520 U.S. 292 (1997).

CURRENT ISSUES INVOLVING MEDICALIZATION, SEXUALITY, GENDER, AND THE LAW

PART A. SCIENCE–BASED QUESTIONS ABOUT THE ASSUMPTION OF SEX BINARINESS

Page 212. Add the following at the end of Part A:

Angela Moreno, as told to Jan Goodwin, "Am I a Woman or a Man?," *Mademoiselle*, March 1998, pp. 178–181, 208. Angela Moreno tells her story. She was born in 1973, with XY chromosomes and internal testes but also had a vagina and clitoris and was raised as a girl. (Fausto–Sterling [casebook, p. 204] would call her a "male pseudohermaphrodite." Money et al. [casebook, p. 205] would call her a "simulant female" case.) When she was 12 years old, her mother noticed that she had a very large clitoris and took her to doctors who performed surgery to cut off part of Angela's clitoris and remove her testes. Angela was told she had ovarian cancer and that the operation was a hysterectomy. Angela recalls her terror and pain after the operation.

"Adolescence, the time of burgeoning sexuality, was a nightmare for me. Every six months, I had to have medical exams, and I began to suspect that what was wrong with me had nothing to do with ovarian cancer. Each time, the doctors obsessively measured my breast development and asked anxiously whether I was dating. I'd tell them I was too busy with school and church, and they'd seem disappointed. They'd keep telling me that I was okay, that I'd have normal sex with my future husband.

"Yet dating, much less marital bliss, was almost impossible for me to imagine then. Once, about a year after surgery, I tried to masturbate—I *was* 13 years old, after all. But, since they had basically amputated my clitoris, I felt no sensation whatsoever. It's no wonder I kept my distance from boys. I didn't even make close friends with girls—I didn't want to explain that I didn't menstruate because I'd had a hysterectomy; I didn't want to ask questions about my body that I couldn't answer. Instead, I put all my energy into studying. I became a straight-A student.

"At the same time, my body—which so fascinated my doctors, and so shamed me—became my enemy. Shortly after the operation, I began to go on food binges, eating potato chips, cookies, and ice cream—and vomiting it all up. Or I'd fast after a binge, then get so hungry that I'd start binging again. My weight swung between 100 and 160 pounds. Before the surgery, I'd never even been chubby." During this tortured adolescence, neither Angela's parents nor her doctors were willing to tell her why the surgery was performed, or that she was an "intersexual," the term she prefers for herself now.

Angela did not know her status until, at age 23, she obtained her medical records. At first she was in shock, then she was enraged that the doctors would have "mutilated" her and no one told her the truth, and then she became self-destructive, binging and purging to the point of exhausted illness. She considered herself a "freak," until she came into contact with the Intersex Society of North America, P.O. Box 31791, San Francisco, California 94131 (ISNA also operates a website–http://www.isna.org), Angela has come to terms with her own body.

Angela says she remains horrified at the doctors' willingness to mutilate her and the lies they told. "I recently confronted an endocriniologist on the Chicago medical team about how she could have considered it ethical to deceive me. She admitted they had doubts, but they were following medical protocol. I asked why they kept reassuring me I'd have normal sex with my future husband. It wasn't *my* sexuality they had in mind—after all, they'd removed my clitoris. What they were really worried about was my being a receptacle for a husband. (I've been a lesbian since I was 21; I've wondered if my orientation comes from being chromosomally male.)"

PART C. HARD-WIRED HOMOSEXUALS?

Page 219—Add the following Note right before the Stein excerpt:

NOTE ON RECENT STUDIES OF THE POSSIBLE BIOLOGICAL ROOTS OF HOMOSEXUALITY

The most recent and sophisticated study using twins to study sexual orientation is J. Michael Bailey, Michael Dunne, and Nicholas Martin, "Sex Differences in the Distribution and Determinants of Sexual Orientation in a National Twin Sample" (1997 Ms.). Bailey et al. report that between 20 and 38% (depending on how broad a notion of being gay or bisexual is used) of the identical twins of gay and bisexual men were also gay or bisexual and that between 24 and 36% of identical twins of gay and bisexual women were also gay or bisexual. This is lower than earlier studies by Bailey and his colleagues (casebook, pp. 217–18); the earlier studies showed that about fifty percent of the identical twins of gay and bisexual people were also gay or bisexual. (Bailey's own assessment of his earlier studies is that the population sample he used may be biased.) The most interesting and consistent finding of recent twin studies is that at least half of identical twins had different sexual orientations. See William Byne & Bruce Parsons, "Sexual Orientation: The Biological Theories Reappraised," 50 *Archives of*

General Psychiatry 228–39 (1993). This is the case even though the identical twins in these studies shared all of their genes and most environmental factors. It is not clear how to use twin studies to disentangle the genetic and environmental influences that operate on identical twins. See Edward Stein, *Sexual Desires: Science, Theory and Ethics* (forthcoming 1999).

Of the biological studies discussed in the casebook, the genetic linkage study by Dean Hamer's group is the most conceptually complex and therefore has properly received the greatest critical attention. Recall that Hamer presents statistical evidence for the proposition that genes influencing sexual orientation may reside in the q28 region of the X chromosome (casebook, p. 218). Hamer found that of 40 pairs of gay siblings, 33 instead of the expected 20 had received the same Xq28 region from their mother. This, he argues, is both surprising and statistically very unlikely to have occurred by chance. His critics are not sure. One criticism is that Hamer's findings have not yet been replicated; a Canadian research team has been unable to duplicate the finding using a comparable experimental design. See Eliot Marshall, "NIH 'Gay Gene' Study Questioned," 268 *Science* 1841 (1995) (discussing Canadian study). Also, Hamer's results may not be statistically significant. Hamer assumed a 2% base rate for homosexuality in the population. If the rate were 4% or higher, as many people believe, then Hamer's results are not statistically significant. Neil Risch, Elizabeth Squires–Wheeler, and Bronya Keats, "Male Sexual Orientation and Genetic Evidence," 262 *Science* 2063 (1993), maintain that Hamer's own data support the 4% estimate.

Scientist William Byne suggests three models for how genes might play a role in one's sexual orientation (see Byne & Parsons, *supra*). Under a *permissive effect model*, genes might influence the neural material on which sexual orientation is inscribed by formative experience. Genetic factors might circumscribe the circumstances upon which experience can effect a person's sexual orientation. Under an *indirect effect model*, genes predispose a person to have temperamental traits that influence how one interacts with and shapes one's environment and formative experiences. On this view, the same genes might predispose the subject to homosexuality in some environments, to heterosexuality in others, and have no effect on sexual orientation in others. Under the *direct effect model*, genes determine neural structures that mediate sexual orientation. The researchers who have most caught the media's attention—Hamer and LeVay—follow this model, which seems least supported by scientific evidence at this point.

Not least importantly, philosophers and scientists are now discussing ethical issues implicated by this new "gay science." See Stein, *Sexual Desires*, above; Udo Schuklenk et al., "The Ethics of Genetic Research" (1997). Among those issues are the following: Are the researchers essentializing homosexuality by the assumptions of their work? (Related is the debate over "How many homosexuals are there?" and the many challenges to the "one in ten" number.) Given the antihomosexual nature of American society, are they not presenting possibilities of "gay genocide" through selective abortions of fetuses with a supposed "gay gene" (for example)?

CHAPTER 3

THEORIES OF SEXUALITY, GENDER AND LAW

SECTION 1

MODERN THEORIES OF SEXUALITY

PART A.   NATURAL LAW THEORIES

Page 234—Add the following new Notes:

NOTE ON NATURAL LAW AS A LITIGATION STRATEGY

John Finnis, whose excerpt you read in the casebook, gave evidence for the state of Colorado in the *Romer* litigation. [See casebook, p. 93.] The State asserted as one of the justifications for Amendment 2 that it expressed the moral judgment of the people of the state. The plaintiffs argued that this expression of "morality" amounted to no more than prejudice, which was not a legitimate state interest. In response to that argument, the defendants introduced Finnis' affidavit, which asserted that anti-homosexual discourse had been part of western philosophy since the ancient Greeks. Finnis' affidavit read in part:[a]

A political community that judges that the stability and educative generosity of family life is of fundamental importance to the communi-

---

a. Excerpt published in "Is Homosexual Conduct Wrong? A Philosophical Ex- change," *The New Republic*, Nov. 15, 1993, p. 12.

ty's present and future can rightly judge that it has a compelling interest in denying that homosexual conduct is a valid, humanly acceptable choice and form of life, and in doing whatever it properly can, as a community with uniquely wide but still subsidiary functions, to discourage such conduct.

The state sought to link this philosophical tradition with contemporary Colorado by citing polling data which showed that the state's residents did not view homosexuality as morally equivalent to heterosexuality. Amendment 2, the state argued, represented the voters' expression of those views.[b]

The state's litigation strategy represented the most serious attempt to date to justify natural law views as deriving from entirely secular roots. Do you think the combination of Plato and polling is persuasive? Implicitly, the state also drew on Finnis's stature as a scholar; he is a professor of law and legal philosophy at Oxford, as well as a law professor at Notre Dame. For good measure, the state also called as a witness Professor Robert George, an associate professor of politics at Princeton University, who is also a lawyer. Will a line-up of respected scholars from prestigious universities affect how courts will assess a morality claim?

As a result of how the parties framed the case, the court heard extensive testimony on the proper interpretation of certain Greek texts.[c] Are there other kinds of cases in which a natural law defense of morality might be more successful than it was in *Romer*?

NOTE ON NATURAL LAW AND MARITAL RELATIONSHIPS

What implications does natural law thinking such as Finnis' have for human sexual and gendered relationships? Natural law valorizes the male-female relationship in a special way, as the foundational relationship for bearing and raising children, and natural law once emphasized the husband as the ruler of the household. It is not clear how natural law thinkers would conceptualize the matter today. Religious natural law thought is diverse.

As the Finnis excerpt suggests (casebook, p. 231), the Roman Catholic Church treats marriage as a *companionate* relationship, where the husband and the wife owe *mutual obligations* to one another. In 1994, the Roman Catholic Bishops in the United States issued a pastoral letter on family life

---

b. See Timothy Tymkovich, "A Tale of Three Theories: Reason and Prejudice in the Battle over Amendment 2," 68 *U. Colo. L. Rev.* 287, 310 (1997).

c. For an account of the fascinating battle of the experts that ensued, complete with accusations of perjury, see Daniel Mendelsohn, "The Stand: Expert Witnesses and Ancient Mysteries in a Colorado Courtroom," *Lingua Franca*, September/October 1996, pp. 34 ff.

which urged "mutual submission" of husband and wife to one another, and joint submission to their children and the family unit.

On June 9, 1998, the Southern Baptist Convention amended its statement of beliefs, the Baptist Faith and Message, to include this declaration:[d]

> The husband and wife are of equal worth before God. Both bear God's image but each in differing ways. The marriage relationship models the way God relates to His people. A husband is to love his wife as Christ loved the church [see Ephesians 5:22–33]. He has the God-given responsibility to provide for, to protect and to lead his family. A wife is to submit graciously to the servant leadership of her husband even as the church willingly submits to the headship of Christ [see *id.*]. She, being "in the image of God" as is her husband and thus equal to him, has the God-given responsibility to respect her husband and to serve as his "helper" in managing the household and nurturing the next generation.

The Faith and Message, originally written in 1925 and rarely amended since, is not binding on Baptists, who stress the individual's personal relationship with God, unmediated by formal churches, but does reflect consensus among the Convention delegates and is supposed to guide seminarians.

Public opinion on these issues is decidedly mixed. A 1998 *Washington Post*/Harvard University poll found the large majority of respondents ambivalent about changes in gender roles since the 1950s.[e] Although most Americans did not subscribe to all of the planks of "traditionalist" attitudes (as defined by the pollsters: husband should be the primary breadwinner, wife should focus on the household and should stay at home if possible), 68% agreed that it would be "better" if the wife could stay at home and take care of the house and children. More than one-third of the respondents thought the country would be better off if men and women returned to the Ozzie-and-Harriet sex roles of the 1950s (42% women, 35% men); about one-third thought the country would be worse off (35% men, 33% women); the rest thought no difference. Men and women rank different goals differently, with men more likely to value career and an active sex life and women more likely to value close friends and relationships with relatives. On the other hand, more Americans think gender roles are socially created than think them biologically determined.[f]

d. Gustav Niebuhr, "Southern Baptists Declare Wife Should 'Submit' to Her Husband," *New York Times*, June 10, 1998, pp. A1, A24.

e. See Kristin Grimsley & R.H. Melton, "Full–Time Moms Earn Respect, Poll Says," *Wash. Post*, Mar. 22, 1998, at A16; Richard Morin & Megan Rosenfeld, "With More Equity, More Sweat," *id.* at A1, A17.

f. Differences between men and women, according to the poll:

	Men	Women
Brought up	44%	55%
Biological make-up	43%	31%
Both equally (volunteered)	11%	12%

NOTE ON ANOTHER KIND OF NATURAL LAW THINKING: SOCIOBIOLOGY

Scientific theories of "sociobiology" start with the proposition that human beings reflect millennia of evolutionary development and derive from that theories of how certain traits are biologically rational adaptations.[g] For sociobiology, "gender" differences may be the result of evolutionary adaptation, rather than just socially constructed roles. Law and economics scholars cited in note "g" maintain that sexual differentiation results from, or is strongly influenced by, the different reproductive roles of men and women: Men, the inseminators, have the ability to engage in rivalrous, aggressive, and promiscuous behavior and not as much incentive to stick around for the rearing of offspring as women, whose pregnancies incapacitate them as well as connect them with their offspring. Natural selection would be expected to favor the generation of females who have a low sex drive and are nurturant and loyal, and males who have a high sex drive and are bold and aggressive (Posner 90–93). Judge Richard Posner notes the similarity of his sociobiological insights and theories of "cultural feminism," such as Carol Gilligan, *In a Different Voice: Psychological Theory and Women's Development* (1982) (women's reasoning tends to be more other-regarding than men's).

These features of sociobiology, as understood by some legal scholars, are subject to argument and dispute; even more controversial are the normative conclusions drawn from it by leading law and economics scholars. Richard Epstein, for example, cautions that "men and women are more comfortable in playing the roles that are congenial to their biological roles, and will find themselves uneasy with powerful social [or legal] conventions that dictate a parity in social roles in courtship, marriage, and parenting" (Epstein 336). Although Epstein (ritually) concedes that nature is not a sure guide to regulation, the general thrust of his and Posner's prescriptive arguments is that legal regulations cutting against the grain of evolutive imperative are doomed to expensive failure, just as are legal regulations cutting against the grain of free markets.

Consider the implications of this kind of thinking for cases introduced in Chapter 1 of the casebook. The VMI Case (pp. 81–90) would seem marginal and wasteful under the assumptions of scholars such as Epstein and, possibly, Posner. If men are sociobiologically more aggressive than women, few women will apply to VMI, and the expenses of accommodating

---

g. Sociobiology classics include Edward O. Wilson, *On Human Nature* (1979), and Richard Dawkins, *The Selfish Gene* (1976). Leading applications of sociobiology to legal regulatory issues include Richard Posner, *Sex and Reason* 88–98, (1992), reviewed by Gillian Hadfield, "Flirting with Science: Richard Posner on the Bioeconomics of Sexual Man," 106 *Harv. L. Rev.* (1992); Richard Epstein, "Two Challenges for Feminist Thought," 18 *Harv. J.L. & Pub. Pol'y* 321 (1995), with a response in Mary Anne Case, "Of Richard Epstein and Other Radical Feminists," *id.* at 369. See also Herma Hill Kay, "Perspectives on Sociobiology, Feminism, and the Law," in *Theoretical Perspectives on Sexual Difference* 74 (Deborah Rhode ed. 1990).

women will seem inefficient. (Note how the sociobiology critique mirrors the Franke critique [casebook, pp. 90–91] of cases like VMI: Franke criticizes the Court for treating sex as natural, when it is socially constructed—like gender. Epstein might criticize the Court for treating gender as socially constructed, when it is to a great extent biological—like sex.)

The implications of sociobiology for cases like *Bowers v. Hardwick* (casebook, pp. 44–53) are more unclear, because sociobiology lacks a good theory of homosexuality. If gay people's relationships do not contribute to the perpetuation of the species, why do people attracted to those of their own sex keep popping up throughout human history? What evolutionary role do they play? Posner reads sociobiology to suggest that homosexuality is a product of the way in which the "best" men will tend to accumulate lots of women, leaving some men without sexual partners, and so they turn to one another (Posner, 99). This explains, according to Posner, why more men than women are gay. Elsewhere in his book on *Sex and Reason*, Posner harshly criticizes *Hardwick*, but on libertarian and even pragmatic grounds rather than sociobiological ones. How would his theory of sexual deviance cut? It might support the *Hardwick* dissenters if read for the proposition that it is wasteful to prosecute male "homosexuals," because they are serving a good evolutionary function. But it might support the majority if constitutional protection would encourage gay people to become more public, and if it were further believed that bisexual adolescents might choose homosexuality en masse. (Counter: but not if homosexuality is hard-wired. Also: if over- rather than underpopulation is the problem, increased homosexuality might be a needed safety valve that could save the species [and the earth] from too many human beings.)

This Note can serve as a bridge between theories of natural law (Part A) and rational choice theories (Part B). Posner's *Sex and Reason* makes each kind of argument, but separately, as he claims that his sociobiology points are completely independent of his economic (rational choice) points.

PART B. MATERIALIST OR ECONOMIC THEORIES

Page 248—Add the following at the end of Part B:

Elisabeth Young–Bruehl, *The Anatomy of Prejudices* (1996). The D'Emilio, Posner, Mill, and Rose theories in Part B of the casebook all focus on the reasons why self-interested, rational people might depart from traditional gender and sexual roles. What most such theory neglects is why self-interested, rational people might be prejudiced against other people. The standard story, classically captured in Gordon Allport, *The Nature of Prejudice* (1954), is that prejudiced people are dysfunctional—emotionally rigid, unconnected from their feelings—in a word, irrational. Elisabeth Young–Bruehl approaches the matter from a rational choice perspective: "There is, in fact, no empirical evidence at all that people who are prejudiced are any more pathological than the general population, and also no evidence that particular pathologies subtend either prejudice as a 'generalized attitude' or specific prejudices. On the contrary, many people have prejudices *instead of* the conventional forms of the various pathologies, somewhat as people have perversions instead of neuroses if they act on their forbidden desires rather than repressing them. It has often been noted that many neurotics 'recover' in terrible social circumstances—in war zones, for example—where the pain of the external world distracts them from the pain of their internal worlds. Participating in a supremacist movement can have a similar effect. It gives people 'real' (to them) targets for hatreds they might otherwise expend on themselves. And it gives them a context in which their hatreds are 'normal' (which may mean, of course, that the *society* is pathological). In 1961, when the political philosopher Hannah Arendt attended the trial of Adolf Eichmann in Jerusalem and pronounced him 'terrifyingly normal,' 'banal,' she raised a storm of controversy, but I think she was quite correct in the sense that Eichmann functioned better in his [Nazi Germany genocidal] bureaucracy than he would have without it." (Pages 32–33.)

Accordingly, Young–Bruehl also rejects the traditional idea that *prejudice* is univocal. Instead, she sees prejudice more complexly: different kinds of prejudices serve different kinds of emotional needs. To take three common prejudices, antisemitism is different from racism, and both are different from sexism. Here's how: "*Obsessional prejudices* [like antisemitism] are the prejudices toward which people who are given to fixed ideas and ritualistic acts gravitate and through which they can behave sadistically without being conscious of their victims—as though in a trance, completely 'in cold blood.' Obsessional characters are cut off from their own feelings," and their prejudices "feature conspiracies of demonic enemies everywhere, omnipresent pollutants, filthy people, which the obsessionally prejudiced feel compelled to eliminate—wash away, flush away, fumigate, demolish." (Page 33, emphasis added.)

"Racism, by contrast, exemplifies *hysterical prejudice*, by which I mean a prejudice that a person uses unconsciously to appoint a group to act out in the world forbidden sexual and sexually aggressive desires that the person has repressed. Racism is a prejudice that represents or symbolizes genital power or prowess and sexual desires by bodily features like skin color, thick hair, muscularity, or big breasts; it equates strength, size, and darkness with primitivity, archaic and unrestrained sexual activity forbidden in 'civilization.' * * * Racism is a prejudice of desire for regression expressed as a charge that people who are 'other' and sexually powerful—as parents and siblings are in the eyes of children—have never progressed, are intellectually inferior, are uncivilized. The 'lower' men are imagined as brutal, the 'lower' women as either (and sometimes both) sexually lascivious or maternally bountiful, milk giving and care giving." (Page 34, emphasis added.) Racist societies are, according to Young–Bruehl, typically split between a formally egalitarian, puritanical facade, and an explosively sexual and aggressive underbelly constantly threatening to break the surface placidity.

"Sexists, finally, are people (usually but certainly not always male) who cannot tolerate the idea that there exist people not like them, not—specifically—anatomically like them. Their prejudice has a *narcissistic* foundation, that is, of the ideologies of desire, the most universal—as universal as narcissism is—even though it is most life defining and extreme in people whose narcisstic desires dominate their character. The narcissistic prejudices of boundary establishment, of genital intactness asserted and mental integrity insisted upon. On the other side of the narcissists' boundaries there is not a 'them,' a 'not-us,' but blank, a lack—or at the most, a profound mystery. Women challenge male gender identity and represent the possibility of castration." (Page 35, emphasis added.) The central mechanism of sexism is control over women's sexuality and reproduction.

Interestingly, Young–Bruehl views homophobia as a synthesis of all three types of prejudice. Unlike many gay and feminist theorists, she refuses to see homophobia as either dysfunctional or univocally sexist. Instead, homophobia is triply functional—it can be *obsessional* for the bigot who sees his own failures as a consequence of homosexual (Jewish, classist) cabals and conspiracies; *hysterical* for the homophobe who is projecting onto others his own disgusting and forbidden fantasies; and *narcissistic* for the person whose own gender identity (masculinity/femininity) is unstable.

Young–Bruehl's is a fascinating theory of prejudices. Does the complexity she brings to an understanding of homophobia also apply to other prejudices? For example, does racism partake of narcissistic or obsessional as well as hysterical elements? How would the author understand prejudice against transsexuals and cross-dressers? Upon what basis should "prejudice" be judged if one believes her claim that it serves emotional "functions"? Does her theory stimulate the same charges leveled against Arendt a generation ago, that she is normalizing evil feelings? How would Young–Bruehl respond?

Consider how her theory illuminates *Hardwick* and the VMI Case from Chapter 1, as well as *Hopkins* and *Rowland* in Chapter 3 of the casebook. (Indeed, can the judicial opinions in *Hardwick* and *Rowland* be read as examples of prejudiced discourse? Reread the Colorado initiative materials reprinted in Chapter 8 of this Supplement: Do they exemplify "prejudiced" discourse associated with homophobia?) Young–Bruehl's theory of prejudices is particularly relevant to the materials in Chapter 4 (military exclusions) and Chapter 7 (education).

PART C.   FEMINIST THEORIES

Page 261. Add the following at the end of Part C:

Robin West, "The Difference in Women's Hedonic Lives: A Phenomenological Critique of Feminist Legal Theory," 3 *Wisconsin*

Women's Law Journal **81 (1987).** This article presents another way feminist theory analyzes sexuality and gender. Professor West starts with this point: "Women's subjective, hedonic lives are different from men's. The quality of our suffering is different from that of men's, as is the nature of our joy." (Page 81.) From this idea, West criticizes both liberal feminism (e.g., that of Justice Ginsburg illustrated in the VMI Case; to some extent, Gayle Rubin's stance as to issues of sexual choice) and radical feminism (e.g., that of Professor MacKinnon and illustrated in her antipornography ordinances). Liberal feminists treat women's problem as lacking choices, and urge that women be given more choices; radical feminists treat women's problem as lacking power, and therefore urge as a solution greater power. Both kinds of theory direct women's thinking outward, to change the world, and thus neglect inwardness strategies of understanding women's needs—the robust insight of feminism's distinct methodology of consciousness-raising.

Like liberalism generally, and rational choice theories such as those explored in Part B of this section of Chapter 3, liberal feminist legal theory starts with the descriptive claim that human beings consent to transactions that maximize their own welfare. But this might be a gendered conception of rationality. "Thus it may be that women generally *don't* consent to changes *so as to* increase our own pleasure or satisfy our own desires. It may be that women consent to changes so as to increase the pleasure or satisfy the desires of *others*. The descriptive account of the phenomenology of choice that underlies the liberal's conceptual defense of the moral primacy of consent may be wildly at odds with the way women phenomenologically experience the act of consent. If it is—if women 'consent' to transactions not to increase our own welfare but to increase the welfare of others—if women are 'different' in this psychological way—then the liberal's ethic of consent, with its presumption of an essentially selfish consensual act, when even-handedly applied to both genders, will have disastrous implications for women." (Page 92.) Recall the game-theoretic feminist argument by Carol Rose in Part B (casebook, p. 248). A consequence of liberal legal feminism, West argues, is that law then "validates" much of the suffering women endure, because they have "chosen" it through marriage, saying yes on a date, and acceding to the advances of a professor or a job supervisor. The fear and coercion that supposedly differentiates rape from sex is so pervasive as to blur the distinction, for many women, beyond liberal recognition, West claims. See, e.g., Del Martin, *Battered Wives* (1984); *Women Against Violence Against Women* (Rhodes & McNeil eds. 1985).

West also criticizes MacKinnon's radical feminism for placing theory ahead of women's experience. Radical legal feminism assumes that equality in power relationships equates with happy and good lives and takes as its project the eradication of any kind of hierarchy, whether or not it is experienced by women as bad or painful (p. 113). The major situs for this gap between theory and experience is *sexuality*. According to MacKinnon, "male dominance and female submission in sexuality *is* the evil: they express as well as *are* women's substantive inequality. But women report—with increasing frequency and as often as not in consciousness-raising sessions—that equality *in sexuality* is not what we find pleasurable or desirable. Rather, the experience of dominance and submission that go with the controlled, but fantastic, 'expropriation' of our sexuality is precisely what *is* sexually desirable, exciting, and pleasurable—in fantasy for many; in reality for some." (Pages 116–17.) See, e.g., Pat Califia, *Sapphistry: The Book of Lesbian Sexuality* (1980); Maria Marcus, *A Taste for Pain: On Masochism and Female Sexuality* (1981). West faults some radical legal feminists for ignoring these reports and insisting that theory obliterate these stories, contrary to consciousness-raising. Note that both West and MacKinnon fail to account for, or even acknowledge, the frequency of female dominance and male submission in the fantasies and experiences of both men and women.

Most deeply, West questions an assumption common to both Rubin and MacKinnon—"the Kantian assumption that *to be human* is to be in some sense autonomous—meaning, minimally, to be differentiated, or individuated, from the rest of social life" (pp. 139–40).

"Underlying and underscoring the poor fit between the proxies for subjective well-being endorsed by liberals and radicals—choice and power—and women's subjective, hedonic lives is the simple fact that women's lives—*because of our biological, reproductive role*—are drastically at odds with this fundamental vision of human life. Women's lives are *not* autonomous, they are profoundly relational. * * * The experience of being human, for women differentially from men, includes the counter-autonomous experience of a shared physical identity between woman and fetus, as well as the counter-autonomous experience of the emotional and psychological bond between mother and infant." (Page 140.) Women's greater responsibility for children also presses women toward greater dependence on others, and relationships with others. Motherhood, and perhaps even its potential, leaves women vulnerable, unequal, and non-autonomous. To the extent that neither MacKinnon nor Rubin starts with this hedonic reality, neither creates a completely satisfying feminist theory of sexuality, gender, and the law.

West argues for a reconception of what "good" sexuality is. Unlike Rubin, she does not ground her theory on consent or choice; unlike MacKinnon, she does not ground her theory on dominance or submission. Her theory is hedonic: what conception of sexuality seems to make women's lives happier (p. 142). Her conclusion: sexuality, including sexual submission, has "erotic *value* when it is an expression of *trust*; is damaging, injurious and painful when it is an expression of *fear*; and is *dangerous* because of its ambiguity; both others and we ourselves have difficulty in disentangling the two" (p. 129).

Quaere: Has West rightly captured women's hedonic experience? If not, have MacKinnon or Rubin? If so, do West's conclusions then follow? Has she essentialized a gendering of sexual roles? Note particularly West's emphasis on women's monopoly on pregnancy, which creates a more relational humanity according to West. This kind of thinking has some affinities to cultural feminism and even to some theories of sociobiology (see the note above). Is it subject to the charge of "false essentialism"? For example, does West adequately capture the experience of lesbians?

SECTION 2

POSTMODERN THEORIES

PART A. SEXUALITY AS A SOCIAL CONSTRUCTION

Page 267—Insert the following after Problem 3–1:

NOTE ON CONSTRUCTIONISM, ESSENTIALISM AND LAW

What are the ramifications of social construction theory? This is a central question for both gender and sexuality, two realms which are usually depicted in popular culture as almost completely naturalized or biological (but see the polling numbers above, p. of this Supplement). "Boys will be boys." "Men are from Mars, women are from Venus." "I've never been attracted to men [women]; I was born gay." "The sex drive." These phrases have power because they capture what we often experience as "truth." But to what extent are these "truths" themselves the products of culture, rather than of nature?

In the 1980s, feminist and queer theorists began to debate essentialism (the belief that gender and/or sexuality is biological and almost entirely predetermined) and social constructionism (the foucauldian argument that gender and sexuality are the products of cultural discourses, i.e. systems of knowledge and power). In the excerpt that follows, Professor Janet Halley describes an essentialist/constructionist continuum for sexuality. Rather than thinking of this problem in dichotomous and all-or-nothing terms, she says, let's specify its different aspects. Drawing on the work of anthropologist Carole S. Vance, Halley argues that there are levels of constructionism. One might agree that a person's sexual acts or her sexual self-identification could vary enormously with historical or cultural context (think of D'Emilio's analysis of the impact of urbanization or World War II), but nonetheless believe that the same hypothetical person would be attracted to men (or women), regardless of time or place or how or whether that desire was manifested. Alternatively, one might believe that the gender of one's object choice could itself be shaped by culture. Halley draws out these and other distinctions.

Halley's article also serves as a foreshadowing of the question of how all these theoretical disputes affect law [see Section 3 of this chapter]. Beginning with the bracketed paragraph on p. 270 of the casebook, she considers the equal protection problem presented by the *Watkins* case—whether *Hardwick* forecloses heightened scrutiny for sexual orientation classifications—from a constructionist/essentialist perspective. She argues that a heavily essentialist approach, i.e., that homosexuality is immutable and central to personhood, actually makes the problem worse, but she does not endorse a completely constructionist approach either. How would you resolve that tension? Has Halley resolved it successfully?

PART C.   DECONSTRUCTIVE THEORY

Page 289—Insert prior to the Sedgwick excerpt:

NOTE ON QUEER THEORY

The phrase "queer theory" does not mean theory about gay people. It denotes a broader intellectual project that treats sexuality as central to history and culture, rather than as a (usually marginal) byproduct. In the opening portion of the Sedgwick excerpt, for example, she argues that homosexuality and its trope (a recurring, defining theme) of the closet shape the meanings of many fundamental cultural dynamics, including the public-private distinction. She goes on to argue that sexuality profoundly influences what we conceive of as knowledge, beginning with the Biblical story of Eve, the apple and the tree of knowledge. Then, using the story of Esther as a contrasting narrative, she describes the instabilities of "knowing" "identity" when that identity is sexual. In the final portion of this excerpt, she offers a new way of thinking about some of the implications of the essentialist/constructionist issues that we addressed earlier. Sedgwick describes a system of two discourses—one universalizing, the other minoritizing—that channel our thinking about both sexuality and gender. Sedgwick's book and its deconstructive methodology have spawned several interesting lines of legal literature, notably Janet Halley, "The Construction of Heterosexuality" (cited and discussed in casebook, p. 304) and Kenji Yoshino, "Suspect Symbols: The Literary Argument for Heightened Scrutiny for Gays," 96 *Colum. L. Rev.* 1753 (1996) (emphasizing the pink triangle, the closet, and the body).

CHAPTER 4

U.S. MILITARY EXCLUSIONS AND THE CONSTRUCTION OF MANHOOD

SECTION 2

THE EXCLUSION OF WOMEN FROM COMBAT

Page 365—Add the following Note at the end of the section:

NOTE ON SEXUAL HARASSMENT OF WOMEN IN THE MILITARY

Although the combat exclusion is the main official discrimination against women in the armed forces, the most significant one is more informal: sexual harassment that is allegedly ignored by the top brass. The "Tailhook" scandal, where women were assaulted by chains of scantily clad men at the annual Tailhook assembly, provoked congressional hearings and promises of reform, but the day-to-day harassment of women ranges from a problem to a disaster (depending on who is evaluating the issue).

Even when alleged harassers are prosecuted, results have been disappointing. Sgt. Major Gene McKinney, the highest ranking enlisted person in the army, was charged with sexually assaulting or propositioning six different women under his command. None of the six women knew each other until after the verdict: not guilty of the six counts of sexual misconduct, but guilty of one count of obstructing an investigation. The complainants were not only shocked and disappointed by the verdicts, but suffered severely for coming forward. Staff Sgt. Christine Fetrow went into the witness protection program because of her charge against McKinney and was sequestered from her family for long periods of time, including Christmas. Other women were shunned by their colleagues at work and even by friends, because of the controversial charges. Sgt. Major Brenda Hoster, who filed the first complaint, left the military entirely because of the hostile environment allegedly created by McKinney. The lesson the women read from the verdicts: "As a female, in a professional status, you shut your mouth, you put up [with the harassment], and that's how you succeed."[a]

McKinney, who denied the allegations and was backed up by testimony from his wife, lost his job as sergeant major and saw his exemplary career in shreds by the end of the trial. And he was convicted of one serious criminal offense. Some argued that his race (African American) played a role in the seriousness with which the accusations were taken.

a. Quoted in Dana Priest, "McKinney Accusers Tell of Hardships—Army Blamed for Failing to Protect Witnesses' Reputation," *Wash. Post*, March 16, 1998, at A1.

SECTION 3

THE MILITARY'S EXCLUSION OF LESBIANS, GAY MEN, AND BISEXUALS

Page 403. Add the following Note before *Thomasson*:

NOTE ON DISCHARGES UNDER THE DON'T ASK, DON'T TELL POLICY

Fiscal Year	Discharges, Gay-Related	Total Active Forces	Discharges as % Total Forces
1980	1754	2,036,672	.086
1981	1817	2,068,885	.088
1982	1998	2,096,644	.095
1983	1815	2,112,067	.086
1984	1822	2,123,428	.086
1985	1660	2,137,415	.078
1986	1644	2,156,593	.076
1987	1380	2,163,578	.064
1988	1100	2,123,669	.051
1989	997	2,115,234	.047
1990	941	2,043,700	.046
1991	949	1,985,500	.048
1992	708	1,807,100	.039
1993	682	1,705,000	.040
1994	597	1,610,400	.037
1995	722	1,523,300	.047
1996	850	1,471,722	.057
1997	997	NA	NA

This data (except for 1997) were compiled by the Servicemembers Legal Defense Network (SLDN) from public figures published by the Defense Department. The data suggest that the number of discharges for gay-related reasons have declined over the last 17 years, both in absolute terms and as a percentage of personnel on active duty; but *the numbers and the percentages have spiked upward since the Clinton Administration's implementation of don't ask, don't tell*. The number of discharges is at its highest level since 1989, and the rate of discharges is at its highest level since 1987. Why is that?

SLDN argues that the numbers have increased, because the Department of Defense (DoD) is not implementing the policy in good faith: military officials are asking, and vigorously investigating, sometimes in the kind of witch-hunts that the president promised would end.[b] In 1996, for example, SLDN documented 89 different violations of the don't ask policy, and established that the official recruiting form still asks recruits if they are "homosexual or bisexual"; the administration's claim that this question is supposed to be marked out is belied not only by the failure of recruiters to do so, but by some recruiters' circling and highlighting this question, without documented reprimand notwithstanding constant complaints by SLDN. In spring 1996, Lieut. Col. Abraham Turner confronted cadet Nicole Galvan about her alleged sexual orientation, in front of four witnesses, and later seized her personal diary, impelling her to resign. In 1997, DoD was castigated by Judge Stanley Sporkin for violating not only the don't ask, don't tell statute, but also the Electronic Communications Privacy Act of 1986, 18 U.S.C. § 2703, when it pressured America Online to reveal the author of an Internet message authored by Navy Senior Chief Timothy McVeigh. See *McVeigh v. Cohen*, 983 F.Supp. 215 (D.D.C.1998). SLDN has documented dozens of other cases where the government violated its own regulations, without any higher-level reprimand or response in the face of repeated and sometimes public complaints. Moreover, DoD officials have investigated and discharged personnel based upon private statements made to medical advisers and even chaplains. DoD has responded to these complaints by making interrogation of suspected personnel's *parents* now optional rather than mandatory. Witch-hunts still focus disproportionately upon female personnel, as in the 1995–1996 witch-hunt of suspected lesbians and gay men on the *USS Simon Lake*, and the 1996 investigations of up to 30 female West Point cadets, including cadet Galvan noted above.

DoD has not responded to all of the SLDN's specific charges, but does maintain that military commanders generally follow the policy of not initiating investigations until there is evidence of "homosexual conduct." DoD also claims that the discharge numbers remain high because soldiers are using the exclusionary policy as an easy exit from the armed forces; however this explanation does not distinguish don't ask, don't tell from the previous, assertedly harsher, policy and seems marginal so long as the country has a volunteer armed forces. In its report on the 1997 discharges, DoD stated that 82% of the 997 discharges involved statements of sexual orientation rather than conduct, but provided no information as to how many of the statements were in connection with witch-hunts and other violations of the don't ask features of the policy.

Neither SLDN nor DoD has a good explanation for *why the percentages have gone up*. Return to theory.

---

b. C. Dixon Osburn & Michelle M. Benecke, *The Third Annual Report on "Don't Ask, Don't Tell, Don't Pursue"* (SLDN, Feb. 26, 1997).

1. *Feminist theory*, including Michelle Benecke's law review article (casebook, pp. 384–88), suggests that the more prominent women become in the armed forces, the more resentful men will resist them, at least for awhile; the time-tested means of woman-bashing in these circumstances is charges of lesbianism. Recall MacKinnon's and Rubin's articles from Chapter 3; both would understand lesbian-baiting as a way that patriarchy (MacKinnon) and sex negativity (Rubin) are enforced in the military.

2. *Prejudice theory*, namely that of Elisabeth Young–Bruehl introduced in Chapter 3 of this Supplement (pp. 42–44), suggests that official "policy" is not going to change people's prejudices if they serve important emotional functions, as homophobia does according to Young–Bruehl. She makes the fascinating observation that the 1993 don't ask, don't tell "compromise" served the interests of *hysterical homophobes* but not other kinds: "Homosexuals may remain in the military, available for actual or fantasy sexual service, but must be secret, closeted. For *obsessionals*, this compromise is a horrible opening of the door to infiltration, an invitation to rapists, and for *narcissists* it is a dreadful blurring of boundaries, a defeat for the project of establishing self-definitional spheres." (Young–Bruehl, *Anatomy of Prejudices* 158–59.) If she is right, then obsessional and narcissistic homophobes might be expected to undermine don't ask, don't tell by continuing to ask, and perhaps by asking with even greater intensity.

3. *Social constructionist theory*, such as Foucault's and Butler's (casebook, pp. 262–82), suggests a related explanation: the high visibility debate about gays in the military itself creates a discourse of silent-but-intense superscrutiny that is more harmful for closeted lesbian and gay personnel than the old policy was. Gay rights advocates themselves have *sexualized* the armed forces in ways that put the unmarried, the slightly unconventional, the loner on the spot in ways that they were not before the public debate. Some military gays believe that the Perry Watkins case (casebook, pp. 109–17) and the 1993 debate among the White House, Congress and the DoD have created a false picture of the armed forces as pervasively sexualized.[c] If that is so, it empowers military homophobes in ways the pre–1993 policy did not, for the homosocial armed forces has a strong incentive in a sex-ambivalent and gay-negative society to purge itself of suspicions of sexual randiness and homosexuality.

Page 405. Add the following Note after *Able*:

NOTE ON DON'T ASK, DON'T TELL CONSTITUTIONAL CHALLENGES, 1997

Thomasson (casebook, pp. 403–04) has emerged as the leading case evaluating the don't ask, don't tell policy, but *Thomasson* and its progeny

---

c. See Jennifer Egan, "Uniforms in the Closet," *New York Times Magazine*, June 28, 1998, at 26–31, 40, 48, 56; Diane Mazur, "The Unknown Soldier: A Critique of 'Gays in the Military' Scholarship and Litigation," 29 *U. Calif. Davis L. Rev.* 223 (1996).

have added little to the analytical debate between the majority and dissent in *Steffan* (casebook, pp. 374–82), a leading pre-don't ask, don't tell precedent. Thus, the Second Circuit (*Able*, casebook, pp. 404–05), Fourth Circuit (*Thomasson*), Eighth Circuit (*Richenberg v. Perry*, 97 F.3d 256 [8th Cir. 1996]), and Ninth Circuit (*Holmes v. California Army Nat'l Guard*, 124 F.3d 1126 [9th Cir.1997]) have basically agreed with Judge Laurence Silberman's analytical structure for disposing of the First Amendment and Equal Protection Clause problems with penalizing a soldier because she says she is gay: the statement "I am gay/lesbian" is not being punished *per se*, but is only being used as evidence that the declarant presumptively commits "homosexual acts" (sodomy) criminal under the Uniform Code of Military Justice [*Steffan*, casebook, p. 377]. Dissenting opinions by Judges K.K. Hall (*Thomasson*), Richard Arnold (*Richenberg*), and Stephen Reinhardt (*Holmes*; compare his dissent in *Watkins*) followed Judge Patricia Wald's *Steffan* dissent in arguing that there is no rational basis for believing that the openly lesbian soldier is *more likely* to engage in illegal behavior than her openly straight male colleague, who is more likely to have engaged in illegal sexual harassment, illegal rape, illegal anal sex and is almost as likely to have engaged in illegal oral sex as well.[d] The circuit court majorities have responded with the deference argument: the armed forces have to make broad categorical judgments, excluding sight-impaired people as well as gays for example, and courts should not interfere with those judgments, especially those that go to the unit cohesion and morale features central to the military mission [*Steffan*, casebook, pp. 376–78]. Recall that the Supreme Court bent over backwards to defer to political and military judgments on an issue of blatant sex discrimination in *Rostker* (casebook, pp. 348–56).

The main twist has been in the Second Circuit. As the casebook says (p. 405), the *Able* panel remanded the case to consider whether the exclusion in § 654(b)(1) of anyone who has committed any "homosexual act" but not any similar "heterosexual act" passes equal protection scrutiny in light of *Romer v. Evans* (casebook, pp. 93–105). Read the following note opinion for the proceedings on remand:

Jane Able et al. v. United States, 968 F.Supp. 850 (E.D.N.Y. 1997). Judge Eugene Nickerson ruled that § 654(b)(1) violates the equal protection component of the Fifth Amendment because it only discharges soldiers for committing sodomy or other sexual contact with someone of the same sex, and not for committing the same activity with someone of the opposite sex. As the statute defines "homosexual act" (§ 654[f][3], casebook, pp. 399–400), a lesbian could be dismissed for kissing another

---

d. The recent University of Chicago study of American sexual patterns found that more than three-quarters of all Americans (straight or gay) have engaged in oral sex, and more than a quarter have engaged in anal sex. Edward Laumann, *Social Organization of Sexuality: Sexual Practices in the United States* 98–99 (1994) (casebook, p. 406). See also Robert Michael et al., *Sex in America* 139–41 (1994).

woman, but a straight woman would not be dismissed for kissing a man—or even for kissing a woman so long as she could show she was really a heterosexual and therefore had no "propensity" for "homosexual acts" (see § 654[b][1][E], casebook, p. 399).

Judge Nickerson found this distinction openly based on third-party prejudices; the government's own rationales for don't ask, don't tell, set forth in the congressional hearings (see casebook, pp. 388–96) and before Judge Nickerson, were grounded in third-party prejudicial reactions to uncloseted gay people (not even to gay people *per se*): the exclusionary policy subserved unit cohesion, protected the privacy of heterosexuals, and reduced sexual tensions in the barracks.

"The private prejudices of heterosexual service members are illegitimate reasons for government-sanctioned discrimination against gay and lesbian service members. See *Romer*. As the Supreme Court, in an opinion by Chief Justice Burger, admonished:

> The Constitution cannot control such prejudices but neither can it tolerate them. Private biases may be outside the reach of the law, but the law cannot, directly or indirectly, give them effect. * * *"

Palmore v. Sidoti, 466 U.S. 429, 433 (1984) [casebook, p. 831]. Judge Nickerson held the statute did precisely what *Palmore* forbade: it directly catered to hysterical heterosexual fears supported by no evidence. "[T]he subjective discomfort, prejudices, and fears of heterosexuals is not a legitimate justification for discrimination against gay men and lesbians. *Romer v. Evans* makes it clear that the Equal Protection Clause prohibits the government from discriminating against one group in order to accommodate the prejudices of another." Judge Nickerson construed the equal protection obligation to preclude the government from pursuing goals that are at root discriminatory and from "indiscriminately imposing inequalities based on naked stereotypes."

Judge Nickerson's ruling might rest on *Evans* alone, that the policy is based on the kind of antigay animus that *Evans* disallowed, but Judge Nickerson also held that antigay discriminations, like those based on sex and race, must satisfy heightened scrutiny. In an analysis similar to that propounded by Judge Norris in *Watkins* (casebook, pp. 110–13) but drawing on a deep study of the academic literature on the history of state discrimination against gay people and the partial state responsibility for the closet,[e] Judge Nickerson found that sexual orientation discrimination met the requirements for heightened scrutiny developed by the Supreme Court: (1)

---

e. E.g., Eve Sedgwick, *The Epistemology of the Closet* (1989); Richard Posner, *Sex and Reason* (1992); William Eskridge, Jr., "Privacy Jurisprudence and the Apartheid of the Closet, 1946–1961," *Fla. St. U.L. Rev.* (1997); Janet Halley, "The Politics of the Closet: Towards Equal Protection for Gay, Lesbian, and Bisexual Identity," 36 *UCLA L. Rev.* 915 (1989); Nan Hunter, "Life After Hardwick," 27 *Harv. C.R.-C.L. L. Rev.* 541 (1992); Kenji Yoshino, "Suspect Symbols: The Literary Argument for Heightened Scrutiny for Gays," 96 *Colum. L. Rev.* 1753 (1996).

there is a strong history of state and private discrimination against gay people, a point not disputed by the government; (2) the discrimination has not been rooted in public-regarding considerations and has repeatedly evinced nothing more than prejudice; and (3) gay people have thereby been marginalized in the political process, along *Carolene* lines (see casebook, preface, pp. xlvi-xlix). Like Judge Norris, Judge Nickerson believed that immutability is not necessary for heightened scrutiny, but that sexual orientation is a significant and hard-to-change part of one's identity.

"The United States has not decided that it is evil to have a homosexual orientation. On the contrary, Congress has determined that homosexuality does not disqualify someone from serving in the Armed Forces. The Act conditions that service on a homosexual's keeping that orientation a secret. It is the very fact that there is bias among heterosexuals in the Armed Forces that led to the Act's requirement that homosexuals remain in the closet." That state of affairs, the judge ruled, is unconstitutional. The government has appealed his ruling to the Second Circuit, and as we go to press the case is pending there.

CHAPTER 5

IDENTITY SPEECH IN THE BODY POLITIC

SECTION 1

POLITICAL SPEECH, PUBLICATION AND ASSOCIATION

PART C. IDENTITY AND VIEWPOINT: THE CLASH OF NONDISCRIMINATION AND FIRST AMENDMENT NORMS

Page 455—Add the following case after the Notes on the Georgetown Case:

NOTE ON STATE AND MUNICIPAL LAWS PROHIBITING SEXUAL ORIENTATION DISCRIMINATION IN PUBLIC ACCOMMODATIONS

The large majority of states and cities have statutes prohibiting discrimination by public accommodations (e.g., hotels, restaurants) on the basis of race, ethnicity, religion, and sex or gender. Seven states also prohibit discrimination by public accommodations on the basis of sexual orientation: Massachusetts (enacted 1989, the statute invalidated in part by *Hurley*, casebook, pp. 438–41), Minnesota (1991), New Hampshire (1997), New Jersey (1991, the statute applied in the *Dale* case below), Rhode Island (1995), Vermont (1991), and Wisconsin (1982). Dozens of cities have similar prohibitions against public accommodation discrimination based on sexual orientation, including Baltimore (ordinance adopted 1988), Boston (1984),

57

Chicago (1988), Cleveland (1984), the District of Columbia (regulation adopted 1973, statute 1977), Detroit (1979), Denver (1990), Los Angeles (1979), New Orleans (1991), New York City (1986), Philadelphia (1982), Portland (1991), St. Louis (1992), San Diego (1990), San Francisco (1978). Most of the statutes and ordinances define "public accommodation" broadly, and this breadth has generated not only questions of statutory interpretation, but also constitutional problems such as that in *Hurley*. Consider the question whether the Boy Scouts can constitutionally be regarded as a "public accommodation" that can be required to admit openly gay scoutmasters. Can the next two decisions be reconciled with one another?

James Dale v. Boy Scouts of America

New Jersey Superior Court, Appellate Division, 1998.
308 N.J.Super. 516, 706 A.2d 270.

■ JUDGE HAVEY

Plaintiff James Dale was expelled from his position as an Assistant Scoutmaster with defendant Monmouth Council, Boy Scouts of America when he publicly declared he was a homosexual. He was expelled by the Boy Scouts of America (BSA) because of its policy excluding avowed homosexuals from membership in its organization. [The court first finds that the BSA is a place of public accommodation under New Jersey's Law Against Discrimination (LAD).] * * *

The trial judge, as an alternative basis for dismissing plaintiff's complaint, held that the First Amendment freedom of association sheltered defendants from the LAD's reach. The judge accepted defendants' assertion that the BSA's fundamental right of freedom of expression permits it to exclude avowed homosexuals who represent and espouse values that are antithetical to boy scout teachings and activities. Defendants' argument, accepted by the trial judge, is that its mission to instill the values of the Scout Oath and Scout Law in boys who join the boy scout troops would be undermined if the state intrudes into its internal affairs by forcing it to accept homosexual members. This contention is predicated on the BSA's policy of excluding avowed homosexuals because homosexuality conflicts with the Scout Oath, demanding that the scout be "morally straight," and the Scout Law, requiring scouts to be "clean." * * *

What emerges from this trilogy of cases [*Roberts* (casebook, pp. 437–38), *Board of Directors of Rotary Int'l v. Rotary Club of Duarte* 481 U.S. 537 (1987) (following *Roberts*), and *New York State Club Ass'n v. City of New York*, 487 U.S. 1 (1988)] is a recognition of the tension between the freedom to associate for the purpose of expressing fundamental views and the compelling state interest in eradicating discrimination. Conciliation of these competing forces is achieved if the state's enforcement of its anti-discrimination law is unrelated to the suppression of ideas and will not "affect in any significant way the existing members' ability to carry out their various purposes." *Board of Dir. of Rotary Int'l*, 481 U.S. at 548. Thus, the organization or club asserting the freedom has a substantial burden of demonstrating a strong relationship between its expressive activities and its discriminatory practice. Any lesser showing invites scuttling of the state's anti-discrimination laws based on pretextual expressive claims.

Will New Jersey's compelling interest in eradicating discrimination by enforcement of the LAD significantly impair the BSA's ability to express its fundamental tenets and to carry out its social, educational and civic activities? For purposes of discussion, we accept the proposition that such goals and activities are protected by the First Amendment freedom of expressive association.

We start with the undisputed fact that the BSA's collective "expressive purpose" is not to condemn homosexuality. Its reason to be is not to provide a public forum for its members to espouse the benefits of heterosexuality and the "evils" of the homosexual lifestyle. As plaintiff convincingly observes, "[b]oys are not urged to join Scouting to learn the 'evils' of being gay, nor are adult leaders recruited to advance some anti-gay agenda." Motivation to advance such anti-gay views was not what "brought [the original members] together."

Rather, a definition of the BSA's mission, purposes and fundamental beliefs is found in its Congressional Charter, bylaws, rules and regulations, and handbooks. The BSA was chartered by Congress with a stated purpose "to promote ... the ability of boys to do things for themselves and others, to train them in Scoutcraft, and to teach them patriotism, courage, self-reliance, and kindred virtues.... " To achieve these goals, the BSA's bylaws provide that emphasis shall be placed upon its "educational program and the oaths, promises and codes of the Scouting program for character development, citizenship training, mental and physical fitness." The BSA's mission is to "serve others by helping to instill values in young people and, in other ways, to prepare them to make ethical choices over their lifetime in achieving their full potential." To that end, the BSA trains and educates boys in camping and other outdoor activities, democracy, civics, respect for the family, personal strength and development, self-sufficiency and sexual responsibility. True to the Scout Oath and Scout Law, adult scout leaders endeavor to impart in the scouts the traditional values of trustworthiness, honesty, independence, physical and moral courage, commitment, cleanliness and fidelity.

We conclude that enforcement of the LAD by granting plaintiff access to the accommodations afforded by scouting will not affect in "any significant way" BSA's ability to express these views and to carry out these activities. On its face, the LAD "does not aim at the suppression of speech nor does it distinguish between prohibited and permitted activity on the basis of viewpoint.... " As applied to the facts before us, it cannot convincingly be argued that the LADs proscription against discrimination based on "affectional or sexual orientation" impedes the BSA's ability to express its collective views on scouting, or to instill in the scouts those qualities of leadership, courage and integrity to which the BSA has traditionally adhered. The LAD does not in any manner require the BSA to abandon or alter any of its laudable activities and programs. The focal point of its prohibition is the act of discrimination against individuals respecting access to public accommodations. Its application here leaves in place the integral workings of the BSA and its constitutional right to carry out its mission.

Indeed, the goals of the BSA are in many respects compatible with the purposes sought to be achieved by the LAD. Its Congressional Charter states that the BSA's bylaws and rules shall not be "inconsistent with the law of the United States of America, or any State thereof...." 36 U.S.C.A. § 22. Such "laws," of course, include anti-discrimination laws. The BSA's publications stress that neither its federal charter nor its bylaws "permits the exclusion of any boy." Consequently, the BSA has a long-term commitment "to a membership that is representative of all economic and racial groups," and encourages its local councils to establish membership that is "representative of the total population of the council or district." (Emphasis added). This commendable quality of inclusion is not at all inconsistent with the purposes of New Jersey's anti-discrimination law.

We reject as irrelevant the trial judge's conclusion that [a]ccording to its mission and purpose, BSA has determined that an assistant scoutmaster who is an active sodomist is simply incompatible with scouting and is not morally "straight." The question here is whether the BSA discriminated against plaintiff because of his "affectional or sexual orientation." The BSA excluded plaintiff because he was an avowed homosexual, not because he was an "active sodomist." The observation also raises, no doubt inadvertently, the sinister and unspoken fear that gay scout leaders will somehow cause physical or emotional injury to scouts, or will instill in them ideas about the homosexual lifestyle. The prevalence of homophobia and stereotypical conceptions of homosexuality within society as a whole, and within the legal system in particular, have been well documented. *Roberts* cautions that, in examining an association's freedom of expressive association claim, "legal decision making that relies uncritically on such [unproven] assumptions" must be condemned. 468 U.S. at 628. Such assumptions, predicated on stereotypical generalizations, rather than fact, cannot be employed as "shorthand measures" in place of legitimate factors justifying First Amendment protection. *New York State Club Ass'n, Inc.*, 487 U.S. at 13.

There is absolutely no evidence before us, empirical or otherwise, supporting a conclusion that a gay scoutmaster, solely because he is a homosexual, does not possess the strength of character necessary to properly care for, or to impart BSA humanitarian ideals to the young boys in his charge. Nothing before us even suggests that a male, simply because he is gay, will somehow undermine BSA's fundamental beliefs and teachings.

Plaintiff's exemplary journey through the BSA ranks is testament enough that these stereotypical notions about homosexuals must be rejected.

Nevertheless, defendants appear to focus on plaintiff's statements as a "gay activist." They claim that his "message," his avowed homosexuality, is "at odds" with scouting's expressive purposes set forth in the Scout Oath and Scout Law. Defendants reason that plaintiff "could hardly be an effective role model for Scouting's morally straight value when he 'stands up' for a view of morality which is inconsistent with that value." * * *

This focus on "morally straight" and "clean" as a basis for excluding avowed homosexual scoutmasters is only of recent vintage. * * * [The court finds that the BSA first declared that homosexual conduct was incompatible with the Scout Oath and Scout Law in 1991, during the pendency of *Curran*, the California case immediately following this one.] It is therefore not unrealistic to view these "Position Statements" as a litigation stance taken by the BSA rather than an expression of a fundamental belief concerning its purposes. * * * [The court also finds that several religious groups that sponsor Boy Scout troops disagree with the anti-gay policy.] What is clear is that the BSA's preemptive exclusion of avowed homosexuals is employed without regard for the diverse ideological differences among the religious institutions and other groups who support the BSA's ideals and activities. As plaintiff and amici persuasively argue, the BSA has not attempted to exclude these religious institutions on the basis that the institutions have condemned the anti-gay policy. Nor has it moved in a wholesale manner to expel heterosexual scouts who have condemned the practice. In contrast, a gay scout leader who says absolutely nothing about the morality or lifestyle of homosexuals is subject to expulsion if he discloses his sexual orientation. These facts belie the BSA's argument that its collective purpose is to "exclude individuals who do not share the views that the club's members wished to promote." *New York State Club Ass'n, Inc.*, 487 U.S. at 13. The facts diminish the BSA's assertion that its policy excluding avowed gays was a collective view that "brought [its members] together." *Roberts*, 468 U.S. at 623.

Defendants argue that because plaintiff's "manifest" views as an avowed homosexual are "at odds" with positions taken by the BSA, plaintiff may be excluded from membership under the United States Supreme Court's holding in *Hurley* [casebook, pp. 438–41]. * * * In our view, *Hurley* is not dispositive here. In *Hurley*, both the Council's parade (reflecting diverse ethnic and social values) and GLIB's desire to participate (to express as a unit its pride in its members' Irish heritage and homosexuality) were expressive activities. As plaintiff observes, both the parade and GLIB's participation were pure forms of speech. To enforce inclusion of GLIB's message in the parade had the effect of altering the expressive context of the speaker's (the Council's) purpose in conducting the parade. Unlike a parade, where the "marchers ... are making some sort of collective point," [*Hurley*, 515 U.S.] at 568, the BSA is a national organization focusing its energy and resources on activities aimed at the physical, moral and spiritual development of boys and young men. The public accommodation law implicated here simply demands access to those activities; it does not attempt, directly or indirectly, to hamper the BSA's ability to carry out these activities or express its views respecting their benefits.

Also, plaintiff is not asserting a right under the LAD to alter the content of the BSA's viewpoint. He merely seeks access to a public accommodation, participation in boy scout activities. His public acknowledgment that he is a homosexual is hardly comparable to a banner in a parade declaring his pride in his homosexuality.

Finally, we cannot accept the proposition that plaintiff's public declaration that he is gay in and of itself constitutes "expressive activity" sufficient to forfeit his entitlement to membership in the BSA. The BSA's argument that this "message" given by plaintiff's declaration conflicts with the BSA "morally straight" and "clean" policies falters, when one considers other scout laws to which scouts promise to subscribe. The scout promises to be "trustworthy," that is, to tell the truth. "Honesty is part of his code of conduct. People can depend always on him." A scout also promises to be "brave," that is, to have the courage "to stand for what he thinks is right even if others laugh at him or threaten him." In our view, there is a patent inconsistency in the notion that a gay scout leader who keeps his "secret" hidden may remain in scouting and the one who adheres to the scout laws by being honest and courageous enough to declare his homosexuality publicly must be expelled. We also cannot accept the proposition that the BSA has a constitutional privilege of excluding a gay person when the sole basis for the exclusion is the gay's exercise of his own First Amendment right to speak honestly about himself. * * *

JUDGE LANDAU, Concurring and Dissenting.

As applied to Dale's status as scoutmaster, I differ with the majority's reliance upon *Roberts v. United States Jaycees*. There, only admission to Jaycee membership was the issue. Of course, the Boy Scouts were not organized for the primary purpose of advancing an anti-gay agenda. However, nothing in *Roberts* prevents an organization from advocating its view that a gay lifestyle is immoral and undesirable without requiring it to provide a platform for competing advocacy, express or implicit. Indeed, as *Hurley* demonstrates, the First Amendment guarantees the Boy Scouts that right of unfettered advocacy.

To the extent the majority opinion questions the fundamental nature of the Boy Scouts' profession of an organizational view on homosexuality, there are two equally dispositive responses. First, it is not for this court to tell the Boy Scouts what to believe or what to profess. That is an internal matter. Their consistent litigation stand in cases like this, and the representations of their governing officials are enough for me. There has been no contravening intervention by opposing Boy Scout groups, although other, non-affiliated, *amici curiae* are abundantly represented in this appeal.

Secondly, when limited to the First Amendment issue of the expressive effect of elevating Dale to an adult leadership role (as distinct from his admission to or retention of Boy Scout membership), whether or not the Boy Scouts' stand on homosexuality is fundamental to that organization's creation is entirely irrelevant.

Based upon the above views, I respectfully dissent from the majority opinion to the extent it would compel the Boy Scouts to accept plaintiff James Dale as assistant scoutmaster or to any Scout leadership position. I concur with the majority result, to the extent that it would require plaintiff be restored to membership.

Curran v. Mt. Diablo Council of the Boy Scouts of America

Supreme Court of California, 1998.
72 Cal.Rptr.2d 410, 952 P.2d 218.

[The opinion of the court held that the Boy Scouts are not a public accommodation within the meaning of California's Unruh Civil Rights Act.]

■ JUSTICE KENNARD, CONCURRING.

* * * This case is unlike those in which the United States Supreme Court has rejected First Amendment challenges to state public accommodation laws by organizations seeking to exclude individuals on grounds unrelated to views advanced by the organizations. In each case, the high court stressed that the law that withstood constitutional scrutiny either "require[d] no change in the [organization's] creed" and "impose[d] no restrictions on the organization's ability to exclude individuals with ideologies or philosophies different from those of its existing members" (*Roberts*), erected no obstacle to "a club seek[ing] to exclude individuals who do not share the views that the club's members wish to promote" (*New York State Club Assn.*), or did "not require the clubs to abandon or alter" any expressive activities (*Bd. of Dirs. of Rotary Int'l*). By contrast, here plaintiff does not share the views promoted by the organization he seeks to join; to require the Boy Scouts to accept him as an assistant scoutmaster would restrict the organization's ability to exclude an individual with a contrary ideology or philosophy.

On point is *Hurley*. * * * The high court's unanimous decision in *Hurley* holding that an organization's right of free speech includes total control over the content of its message and that an organization's right of expressive association allows it to exclude applicants with "manifest views" at odds with those of the organization, is binding on this court. The breadth of the *Hurley* decision raises grave doubts whether California's Legislature could ever constitutionally enact, or this court enforce, a law requiring an organization like the Boy Scouts, whose mission is to instill in boys a certain philosophy of moral behavior, to admit an individual who advances contrary views.[1]

Thus, I agree with Professor William N. Eskridge of Georgetown University Law Center that the high court's decision in *Hurley* dictates a cautious approach to construing antidiscrimination laws. As he puts it: "General antidiscrimination statutes will not be read expansively, beyond their clear application, when the broad reading would directly burden protected First Amendment rights. Such a clear statement rule not only would ameliorate clashes between nondiscrimination and free speech norms but would appropriately place the burden on the legislature to consider First Amendment values when it adopts antidiscrimination laws." (Eskridge, A Jurisprudence of "Coming Out": Religion, Homosexuality, and Collisions of Liberty and Equality in American Public Law (1997) 106 *Yale L.J.* 2411, 2462–2463.)

Here, by construing the term "business establishment" in the Unruh Act as not encompassing the membership and policy decisions of the Boy Scouts, we avoid a statutory construction that could bring the Act's antidiscrimination provisions into conflict with the free speech and expressive association rights that the Boy Scouts and its members have under the First Amendment. * * *

Could the NAACP be compelled to accept as a member a Ku Klux Klansman? Could B'nai B'rith be required to admit an anti-Semite? If the First Amendment protects the membership decisions of these groups, must it not afford the same protection to the membership decisions of the Boy Scouts?

I have grave doubts that the First Amendment permits the state to compel an organization like the Boy Scouts to accept as members those who espouse contrary views. For this reason, as well as those expressed in the majority opinion, I agree that the Boy Scouts of America is not a "business establishment" whose membership and policy decisions are within the reach of the Unruh Act.

---

1. I am not persuaded otherwise by a recent decision of the Appellate Division of the New Jersey Superior Court [*Dale*]. * * * Among the *Dale* majority's reasons for its holding was its rejection of the proposition "that the [Boy Scouts of America] has a constitutional privilege of excluding a gay person when the sole basis for the exclusion is the gay's exercise of his own First Amendment right to speak honestly about himself." But when an individual seeks to use state power to force a private organization to accept that individual as a member, and the individual's views are diametrically opposed to those of the organization, the First Amendment rights at issue are those of the organization and its members, not those of the applicant. Accordingly, the critical issue, which the *Dale* majority never considered, was this: Whether granting the plaintiff the relief he sought would violate the First Amendment right of the Boy Scouts, by means of its policy and membership decisions, to choose the content of the organization's own message. * * *

NOTES ON THE BOY SCOUT CASES

1. *Rights in Conflict.* Are Boy Scout troops more like a Jaycees club or the St. Patrick's Day parade? If the Jaycees had argued that "business is for guys" was part of its "creed," would its exclusion of women members have been preserved? Should courts get involved in assessing the legitimacy of what an organization claims as its creed? Or is that degree of intrusiveness unavoidable if an organization asserts a creed-based defense? The Boy Scouts assert that having openly gay participants is contrary to the oath and rules, but not that the group promotes anti-gay beliefs. Isn't that very similar to the claim made by the organizers of the St. Patrick's Day parade?

2. *Expressive Identity.* Once again, these cases raise the question of whether the simple presence of an openly gay person amounts to expression of a particular viewpoint. Justice Kennard and Judge Landau assume that it does. Judge Havey's opinion for the New Jersey court distinguishes *Hurley* on the ground that Dale's "public acknowledgment that he is a homosexual is hardly comparable to a banner in a parade declaring his pride in his homosexuality." Isn't that precisely the question? What did the banner say that the gay group wanted to carry in the St. Patrick's parade?

3. *A Khaki Ceiling?* The New Jersey court divides on the question of what can be analogized to access to an entity open to the public. The majority treats both Scout membership and a Scout leader position as falling within that rubric. Judge Landau separates the two, and would order the Scouts to admit gay members, but allow the exclusion of gay scoutmasters. In essence, there would be a level of scouting beyond which gay scouts could not go. Does this solve the viewpoint problem? If it does, what are its ramifications beyond the Scouts?

Page 462—Add the following case after *Rosenberger* and the Note:

Gay Lesbian Bisexual Alliance v. Pryor, et al., 110 F.3d 1543 (11th Cir.1997). Section 16–1–28 of the Alabama Code provides:

(a) No public funds or public facilities shall be used by any college or university to, directly or indirectly, sanction, recognize, or support the activities or existence of any organization or group that fosters or promotes a lifestyle or actions prohibited by the sodomy and sexual misconduct laws * * * [Alabama's sodomy law applies to both heterosexual and homosexual acts.]

(b) No organization or group that receives public funds or uses public facilities, directly or indirectly, at any college or university shall permit or encourage its members or encourage other persons to engage in any such unlawful acts or provide information or materials that explain how such acts may be engaged in or performed.

(c) This section * * * shall not apply to any organization or group whose activities are limited solely to the political advocacy of a change in the sodomy and sexual misconduct laws of this state.

Gay Lesbian Bisexual Alliance (GLBA), a student group at the University of South Alabama ("USA"), was denied funding based on the statute. Like the Gay Students Organization in *Bonner* (casebook, pp. 420–24), GLBA sued for funding. (How are the two cases different?)

The court found that USA's system for funding student groups created a limited public forum, and as such, was bound by *Rosenberger*. "USA prohibited funding to GLBA based on the Attorney General's unsupported assumption that GLBA fosters or promotes a violation of the sodomy or sexual misconduct laws. The statute discriminates against one particular viewpoint because state funding of groups which foster or promote compliance with the sodomy or sexual misconduct laws remains permissible. This is blatant viewpoint discrimination."

Quaere: Under *Rosenberger*, is there any strategy Alabama can follow to assure that state monies will not be used by gay student groups? Consider *National Endowment for the Arts v. Finley*, 118 S.Ct. 2168 (1998), which is excerpted in Chapter 6 of this Supplement. Note the *Finley* Court's treatment of *Rosenberger*. Does it cast doubt on the analysis or result in *GLBA* or *Bonner*?

PRIVACY AND SEXUAL "OUTING"

PART C.   DEFAMATION

Page 485—Add to Note 3:

Taking exactly the opposite approach from the North Carolina court in *Hunter*, the Fifth Circuit ruled that calling someone a "faggot" was slander *per se*, despite the fact that the Texas legislature had reduced the crime of sodomy to a misdemeanor, so that it was no longer punishable by imprisonment. *Plumley v. Landmark Chevrolet, Inc.*, 122 F.3d 308, 310 (5th Cir. 1997).

*

CHAPTER 6

Sexual Speech

section 3

Cutting Edge Issues of Sexual Speech Law

Part B.   Censorship of State-Subsidized Speech

Page 579–Substitute the following for the Ninth Circuit decision in *Finley*:

National Endowment for the Arts, et al., v. Karen Finley, et al.

Supreme Court of the United States, 1998.
___ U.S. ___, 118 S.Ct. 2168, ___ L.Ed.2d ___.

■ Justice O'Connor delivered the opinion of the Court.

The National Foundation on the Arts and Humanities Act, as amended in 1990, requires the Chairperson of the National Endowment for the Arts (NEA) to ensure that "artistic excellence and artistic merit are the criteria by which [grant] applications are judged, taking into consideration general standards of decency and respect for the diverse beliefs and values of the American public." 20 U.S.C. § 954(d)(1). In this case, we review the Court of Appeals' determination that § 954(d)(1), on its face, impermissibly discriminates on the basis of viewpoint and is void for vagueness under the First and Fifth Amendments. We conclude that § 954(d)(1) is facially valid, as it neither inherently interferes with First Amendment rights nor violates constitutional vagueness principles.

* * * The four individual respondents in this case, Karen Finley, John Fleck, Holly Hughes, and Tim Miller, are performance artists who applied for NEA grants before § 954(d)(1) was enacted. An advisory panel recommended approval of respondents' projects, both initially and after receiving Frohnmayer's request to reconsider three of the applications. A majority of the Council subsequently recommended disapproval, and in June 1990, the NEA informed respondents that they had been denied funding. Respondents filed suit, alleging that the NEA had violated their First Amendment rights by rejecting the applications on political grounds, had failed to follow statutory procedures by basing the denial on criteria other than those set forth in the NEA's enabling statute, and had breached the confidentiality of their grant applications through the release of quotations to the press, in violation of the Privacy Act of 1974, 5 U.S.C. § 552(a). Respondents sought restoration of the recommended grants or reconsideration of their applications, as well as damages for the alleged Privacy Act violations. When Congress enacted § 954(d)(1), respondents, now joined by the National Association of Artists' Organizations (NAAO), amended their complaint to challenge the provision as void for vagueness and impermissibly viewpoint based.

* * * Respondents argue that the provision is a paradigmatic example of viewpoint discrimination because it rejects any artistic speech that either fails to respect mainstream values or offends standards of decency. The premise of respondents' claim is that § 954(d)(1) constrains the agency's ability to fund certain categories of artistic expression. The NEA, however, reads the provision as merely hortatory, and contends that it stops well short of an absolute restriction. Section 954(d)(1) adds "considerations" to the grant-making process; it does not preclude awards to projects that might be deemed "indecent" or "disrespectful," nor place conditions on grants, or even specify that those factors must be given any particular weight in reviewing an application. Indeed, the agency asserts that it has adequately implemented § 954(d)(1) merely by ensuring the representation of various backgrounds and points of view on the advisory panels that analyze grant applications. We do not decide whether the NEA's view—that the formulation of diverse advisory panels is sufficient to comply with Congress' command—is in fact a reasonable reading of the statute. It is clear, however, that the text of § 954(d)(1) imposes no categorical requirement. The advisory language stands in sharp contrast to congressional efforts to prohibit the funding of certain classes of speech. When Congress has in fact intended to affirmatively constrain the NEA's grant-making authority, it has done so in no uncertain terms. See § 954(d)(2) ("[O]bscenity is without artistic merit, is not protected speech, and shall not be funded").

* * * That § 954(d)(1) admonishes the NEA merely to take "decency and respect" into consideration, and that the legislation was aimed at reforming procedures rather than precluding speech, undercut respondents' argument that the provision inevitably will be utilized as a tool for invidious viewpoint discrimination. * * * Thus, we do not perceive a realistic danger that § 954(d)(1) will compromise First Amendment values. As respondents' own arguments demonstrate, the considerations that the provision introduces, by their nature, do not engender the kind of directed viewpoint discrimination that would prompt this Court to invalidate a statute on its face. Respondents assert, for example, that "[o]ne would be hard-pressed to find two people in the United States who could agree on what the 'diverse beliefs and values of the American public' are, much less on whether a particular work of art 'respects' them"; and they claim that " '[d]ecency' is likely to mean something very different to a septegenarian in Tuscaloosa and a teenager in Las Vegas." The NEA likewise views the considerations enumerated in § 954(d)(1) as susceptible to multiple interpretations. Accordingly, the provision does not introduce considerations that, in practice, would effectively preclude or punish the expression of particular views. Indeed, one could hardly anticipate how "decency" or "respect" would bear on grant applications in categories such as funding for symphony orchestras.

Respondents' claim that the provision is facially unconstitutional may be reduced to the argument that the criteria in § 954(d)(1) are sufficiently subjective that the agency could utilize them to engage in viewpoint discrimination. Given the varied interpretations of the criteria and the vague exhortation to "take them into consideration," it seems unlikely that this provision will introduce any greater element of selectivity than the determination of "artistic excellence" itself. * * *

* * * Any content-based considerations that may be taken into account in the grant-making process are a consequence of the nature of arts funding. The NEA has limited resources and it must deny the majority of the grant applications that it receives, including many that propose "artistically excellent" projects. The agency may decide to fund particular projects for a wide variety of reasons, "such as the technical proficiency of the artist, the creativity of the work, the anticipated public interest in or appreciation of the work, the work's contemporary relevance, its educational value, its suitability for or appeal to special audiences (such as children or the disabled), its service to a rural or isolated community, or even simply that the work could increase public knowledge of an art form." Brief for Petitioners 32. As the dissent below noted, it would be "impossible to have a highly selective grant program without denying money to a large amount of constitutionally protected expression." 100 F.3d, at 685 (Kleinfeld, J., dissenting). * * *

Respondent's reliance on our decision in *Rosenberger v. Rector and Visitors of Univ. of Va.*, 515 U.S. 819 (1995) [casebook, p. 455], is therefore misplaced. In *Rosenberger*, a public university declined to authorize disbursements from its Student Activities Fund to finance the printing of a Christian student newspaper. We held that by subsidizing the Student Activities Fund, the University had created a limited public forum, from which it impermissibly excluded all publications with religious editorial viewpoints. *Id.*, at 837. Although the scarcity of NEA funding does not distinguish this case from *Rosenberger*, see *id.*, at 835, the competitive process according to which the grants are allocated does. In the context of arts funding, in contrast to many other subsidies, the Government does not indiscriminately "encourage a diversity of views from private speakers," *id.*, at 834. The NEA's mandate is to make aesthetic judgments, and the inherently content-based "excellence" threshold for NEA support sets it apart from the subsidy at issue in Rosenberger—which was available to all student organizations that were " 'related to the educational purpose of the University,' "*id.*, at 824 * * *

Respondents do not allege discrimination in any particular funding decision. [Two of the individual plaintiffs received fellowships in September, 1991.] Thus, we have no occasion here to address an as-applied challenge in a situation where the denial of a grant may be shown to be the product of invidious viewpoint discrimination. If the NEA were to leverage its power to award subsidies on the basis of subjective criteria into a penalty on disfavored viewpoints, then we would confront a different case. We have stated that, even in the provision of subsidies, the Government may not "ai[m] at the suppression of dangerous ideas," *Regan [v. Taxation with Representation of Wash.*, 461 U.S. 540, 550 (1983)], and if a subsidy were "manipulated" to have a "coercive effect," then relief could be appropriate. See *Arkansas Writers' Project, Inc. v. Ragland*, 481 U.S. 221, 237 (1987) (Scalia, J., dissenting) * * * In addition, as the NEA itself concedes, a more pressing constitutional question would arise if government funding resulted in the imposition of a disproportionate burden calculated to drive "certain ideas or viewpoints from the marketplace." *Simon & Schuster, Inc. v. Members of N.Y. State Crime Victims Bd.*, 502 U.S. 105, 116 (1991). Unless and until § 954(d)(1) is applied in a manner that raises concern about the suppression of disfavored viewpoints, however, we uphold the constitutionality of the provision.

Finally, although the First Amendment certainly has application in the subsidy context, we note that the Government may allocate competitive funding according to criteria that would be impermissible were direct regulation of speech or a criminal penalty at stake. So long as legislation does not infringe on other constitutionally protected rights, Congress has wide latitude to set spending priorities. See *Regan.* * * *

* * * The terms of the provision are undeniably opaque, and if they appeared in a criminal statute or regulatory scheme, they could raise substantial vagueness concerns. It is unlikely, however, that speakers will be compelled to steer too far clear of any "forbidden area" in the context of

grants of this nature. We recognize, as a practical matter, that artists may conform their speech to what they believe to be the decision-making criteria in order to acquire funding. But when the Government is acting as patron rather than as sovereign, the consequences of imprecision are not constitutionally severe.

In the context of selective subsidies, it is not always feasible for Congress to legislate with clarity. Indeed, if this statute is unconstitutionally vague, then so too are all government programs awarding scholarships and grants on the basis of subjective criteria such as "excellence." To accept respondents' vagueness argument would be to call into question the constitutionality of these valuable government programs and countless others like them.

Section 954(d)(1) merely adds some imprecise considerations to an already subjective selection process. It does not, on its face, impermissibly infringe on First or Fifth Amendment rights.

■ JUSTICE SCALIA, with whom JUSTICE THOMAS joins, concurring in the judgment.

"The operation was a success, but the patient died." What such a procedure is to medicine, the Court's opinion in this case is to law. It sustains the constitutionality of 20 U.S.C. § 954(d)(1) by gutting it. The most avid congressional opponents of the provision could not have asked for more. I write separately because, unlike the Court, I think that § 954(d)(1) must be evaluated as written, rather than as distorted by the agency it was meant to control. By its terms, it establishes content-and viewpoint-based criteria upon which grant applications are to be evaluated. And that is perfectly constitutional.

I

The Statute Means What It Says

* * * The [NEA] application reviewers must take into account "general standards of decency" and "respect for the diverse beliefs and values of the American public" when evaluating artistic excellence and merit. One can regard this as either suggesting that decency and respect are elements of what Congress regards as artistic excellence and merit, or as suggesting that decency and respect are factors to be taken into account in addition to artistic excellence and merit. But either way, it is entirely, 100% clear that decency and respect are to be taken into account in evaluating applications.

This is so apparent that I am at a loss to understand what the Court has in mind (other than the gutting of the statute) when it speculates that the statute is merely "advisory." General standards of decency and respect for Americans' beliefs and values must (for the statute says that the Chairperson "shall ensure" this result) be taken into account (see, e.g., American Heritage Dictionary 402 (3d ed.1992): "consider . . . [t]o take into account; bear in mind") in evaluating all applications. This does not mean that those factors must always be dispositive, but it does mean that they must always be considered. The method of compliance proposed by the National Endowment for the Arts (NEA)—selecting diverse review panels of artists and nonartists that reflect a wide range of geographic and cultural perspectives—is so obviously inadequate that it insults the intelligence. A diverse panel membership increases the odds that, if and when the panel takes the factors into account, it will reach an accurate assessment of what they demand. But it in no way increases the odds that the panel will take the factors into consideration—much less ensures that the panel will do so, which is the Chairperson's duty under the statute. Moreover, the NEA's fanciful reading of § 954(d)(1) would make it wholly superfluous. Section 959(c) already requires the Chairperson to "issue regulations and establish procedures ... to ensure that all panels are composed, to the extent practicable, of individuals reflecting ... diverse artistic and cultural points of view."

* * * [T]he presence of the "tak[e] into consideration" clause "cannot be regarded as mere surplusage; it means something," *Potter v. United States*, 155 U.S. 438, 446 (1894). And the "something" is that the decision-maker, all else being equal, will favor applications that display decency and respect, and disfavor applications that do not.

This unquestionably constitutes viewpoint discrimination. That conclusion is not altered by the fact that the statute does not "compe[l]" the denial of funding, any more than a provision imposing a five-point handicap on all black applicants for civil service jobs is saved from being race discrimination by the fact that it does not compel the rejection of black applicants. If viewpoint discrimination in this context is unconstitutional (a point I shall address anon), the law is invalid unless there are some situations in which the decency and respect factors do not constitute viewpoint discrimination. And there is none. The applicant who displays "decency," that is, "[c]onformity to prevailing standards of propriety or modesty," American Heritage Dictionary 483 (3d ed.1992) (def.2), and the applicant who displays "respect," that is, "deferential regard," for the diverse beliefs and values of the American people, id., at 1536 (def.1), will always have an edge over an applicant who displays the opposite. And finally, the conclusion of viewpoint discrimination is not affected by the fact that what constitutes "decency" or "the diverse beliefs and values of the American people" is difficult to pin down, any more than a civil-service preference in favor of those who display "Republican-party values" would be rendered nondiscriminatory by the fact that there is plenty of room for argument as to what Republican-party values might be. * * *

II

What The Statute Says Is Constitutional

* * * With the enactment of § 954(d)(1), Congress did not abridge the speech of those who disdain the beliefs and values of the American public, nor did it abridge indecent speech. Those who wish to create indecent and disrespectful art are as unconstrained now as they were before the enactment of this statute. Avant-garde artistes such as respondents remain entirely free to *epater les bourgeois*; they are merely deprived of the additional satisfaction of having the bourgeoisie taxed to pay for it. It is preposterous to equate the denial of taxpayer subsidy with measures " 'aimed at the suppression of dangerous ideas.' " *Regan v. Taxation with Representation of Wash.*, 461 U.S. 540, 550 (1983) * * * "The reason that denial of participation in a tax exemption or other subsidy scheme does not necessarily 'infringe' a fundamental right is that—unlike direct restriction or prohibition—such a denial does not, as a general rule, have any significant coercive effect." *Arkansas Writers' Project, Inc. v. Ragland*, 481 U.S. 221, 237 (1987) (Scalia, J., dissenting).

* * * Respondents, relying on *Rosenberger v. Rector and Visitors of Univ. of Va.*, argue that viewpoint-based discrimination is impermissible unless the government is the speaker or the government is "disburs[ing] public funds to private entities to convey a governmental message." [515 U.S. at 833.] It is impossible to imagine why that should be so; one would think that directly involving the government itself in the viewpoint discrimination (if it is unconstitutional) would make the situation even worse. Respondents are mistaken. It is the very business of government to favor and disfavor points of view on (in modern times, at least) innumerable subjects—which is the main reason we have decided to elect those who run the government, rather than save money by making their posts hereditary. And it makes not a bit of difference, insofar as either common sense or the Constitution is concerned, whether these officials further their (and, in a democracy, our) favored point of view by achieving it directly (having government-employed artists paint pictures, for example, or government-employed doctors perform abortions); or by advocating it officially (establishing an Office of Art Appreciation, for example, or an Office of Voluntary Population Control); or by giving money to others who achieve or advocate it (funding private art classes, for example, or Planned Parenthood). None of this has anything to do with abridging anyone's speech. *Rosenberger*, as the Court explains, found the viewpoint discrimination unconstitutional, not because funding of "private" speech was involved, but because the government had established a limited public forum—to which the NEA's granting of highly selective (if not highly discriminating) awards bears no resemblance.

The nub of the difference between me and the Court is that I regard the distinction between "abridging" speech and funding it as a fundamental divide, on this side of which the First Amendment is inapplicable. The Court, by contrast, seems to believe that the First Amendment, despite its words, has some ineffable effect upon funding, imposing constraints of an indeterminate nature which it announces (without troubling to enunciate any particular test) are not violated by the statute here—or, more accurately, are not violated by the quite different, emasculated statute that it imagines. "[T]he Government," it says, "may allocate competitive funding according to criteria that would be impermissible were direct regulation of speech or a criminal penalty at stake." The government, I think, may allocate both competitive and noncompetitive funding *ad libitum*, insofar as the First Amendment is concerned. * * *

■ JUSTICE SOUTER, dissenting.

* * * The decency and respect proviso mandates viewpoint-based decisions in the disbursement of government subsidies, and the Government has wholly failed to explain why the statute should be afforded an exemption from the fundamental rule of the First Amendment that viewpoint discrimination in the exercise of public authority over expressive activity is unconstitutional. * * *

* * * The constitutional protection of artistic works turns not on the political significance that may be attributable to such productions, though they may indeed comment on the political, but simply on their expressive character, which falls within a spectrum of protected "speech" extending outward from the core of overtly political declarations. Put differently, art is entitled to full protection because our "cultural life," just like our native politics, "rests upon [the] ideal" of governmental viewpoint neutrality. *Turner Broadcasting System, Inc. v. FCC*, 512 U.S. 622, 641 (1994).

When called upon to vindicate this ideal, we characteristically begin by asking "whether the government has adopted a regulation of speech because of disagreement with the message it conveys. The government's purpose is the controlling consideration." *Ward v. Rock Against Racism*, [491 U.S.] at 791. The answer in this case is damning. One need do nothing more than read the text of the statute to conclude that Congress's purpose in imposing the decency and respect criteria was to prevent the funding of art that conveys an offensive message; the decency and respect provision on its face is quintessentially viewpoint based, and quotations from the Congressional Record merely confirm the obvious legislative purpose. * * * Indeed, if there were any question at all about what Congress had in mind, a definitive answer comes in the succinctly accurate remark of the proviso's author, that the bill "add[s] to the criteria of artistic excellence and artistic merit, a shell, a screen, a viewpoint that must be constantly taken into account."

* * * "Sexual expression which is indecent but not obscene is protected by the First Amendment," *Sable Communications of Cal., Inc. v. FCC*, 492 U.S. 115, 126 (1989), and except when protecting children from exposure to indecent material, see *FCC v. Pacifica Foundation*, 438 U.S. 726 (1978), the First Amendment has never been read to allow the government to rove around imposing general standards of decency, see, e.g., *Reno v. American Civil Liberties Union*, 521 U.S. ___ (1997) (striking down on its face a statute that regulated "indecency" on the Internet). Because "the normal definition of 'indecent' . . . refers to nonconformance with accepted standards of morality," *FCC v. Pacifica Foundation, supra,*

at 740, restrictions turning on decency, especially those couched in terms of "general standards of decency," are quintessentially viewpoint based: they require discrimination on the basis of conformity with mainstream mores. The Government's contrary suggestion that the NEA's decency standards restrict only the "mode, form, or style" of artistic expression, not the underlying viewpoint or message may be a tempting abstraction * * * But here it suffices to realize that "mode, form, or style" are not subject to abstraction from artistic viewpoint, and to quote from an opinion just two years old: "In artistic ... settings, indecency may have strong communicative content, protesting conventional norms or giving an edge to a work by conveying otherwise inexpressible emotions. ...Indecency often is inseparable from the ideas and viewpoints conveyed, or separable only with loss of truth or expressive power." *Denver Area Ed. Telecommunications Consortium, Inc. v. FCC*, 518 U.S. 727, 805 (1996) (Kennedy, J., joined by Ginsburg, J., concurring) * * *

* * * Just as the statute cannot be read as anything but viewpoint based, or as requiring nothing more than diverse review panels, it cannot be read as tolerating awards to spread indecency or disrespect, so long as the review panel, the National Council on the Arts, and the Chairperson have given some thought to the offending qualities and decided to underwrite them anyway. * * * What if the statute required a panel to apply criteria "taking into consideration the centrality of Christianity to the American cultural experience," or "taking into consideration whether the artist is a communist," or "taking into consideration the political message conveyed by the art," or even "taking into consideration the superiority of the white race"? Would the Court hold these considerations facially constitutional, merely because the statute had no requirement to give them any particular, much less controlling, weight? I assume not. In such instances, the Court would hold that the First Amendment bars the government from considering viewpoint when it decides whether to subsidize private speech, and a statute that mandates the consideration of viewpoint is quite obviously unconstitutional.

* * * The Government freely admits * * * that it neither speaks through the expression subsidized by the NEA, [nor purchases] anything for itself with its NEA grants. On the contrary, believing that "[t]he arts ... reflect the high place accorded by the American people to the nation's rich cultural heritage," § 951(6), and that "[i]t is vital to a democracy ... to provide financial assistance to its artists and the organizations that support their work," § 951(10), the Government acts as a patron, financially underwriting the production of art by private artists and impresarios for independent consumption. Accordingly, the Government would have us liberate government-as-patron from First Amendment strictures not by placing it squarely within the categories of government-as-buyer or government-as-speaker, but by recognizing a new category by analogy to those accepted ones. The analogy is, however, a very poor fit, and this patronage falls embarrassingly on the wrong side of the line between government-as-buyer or-speaker and government-as-regulator-of-private-speech.

* * * Our most thorough statement of these principles is found in the recent case of *Rosenberger v. Rector and Visitors of Univ. of Va.*, which held that the University of Virginia could not discriminate on viewpoint in underwriting the speech of student-run publications. We recognized that the government may act on the basis of viewpoint "when the State is the speaker" or when the state "disburses public funds to private entities to convey a governmental message." 515 U.S. at 833. But we explained that the government may not act on viewpoint when it "does not itself speak or subsidize transmittal of a message it favors but instead expends funds to encourage a diversity of views from private speakers." *Id.*, at 834. When the government acts as patron, subsidizing the expression of others, it may not prefer one lawfully stated view over another.

Rosenberger controls here. The NEA, like the student activities fund in Rosenberger, is a subsidy scheme created to encourage expression of a diversity of views from private speakers. * * * Given this congressional choice to sustain freedom of expression, *Rosenberger* teaches that the First Amendment forbids decisions based on viewpoint popularity. So long as Congress chooses to subsidize expressive endeavors at large, it has no business requiring the NEA to turn down funding applications of artists and exhibitors who devote their "freedom of thought, imagination, and inquiry" to defying our tastes, our beliefs, or our values. * * *

The Court says otherwise, claiming to distinguish *Rosenberger* on the ground that the student activities funds in that case were generally available to most applicants, whereas NEA funds are disbursed selectively and competitively to a choice few. But the Court in *Rosenberger* anticipated and specifically rejected just this distinction when it held in no uncertain terms that "[t]he government cannot justify viewpoint discrimination among private speakers on the economic fact of scarcity." 515 U.S., at 835. Scarce money demands choices, of course, but choices "on some acceptable [viewpoint] neutral principle," like artistic excellence and artistic merit; "nothing in our decision[s] indicate[s] that scarcity would give the State the right to exercise viewpoint discrimination that is otherwise impermissible." *Ibid.* * * *

* * * The Court does not strike down the proviso, however. Instead, it preserves the irony of a statutory mandate to deny recognition to virtually any expression capable of causing offense in any quarter as the most recent manifestation of a scheme enacted to "create and sustain . . . a climate encouraging freedom of thought, imagination, and inquiry." § 951(7).

PART C. "INDECENCY" AND ELECTRONIC MEDIA

Page 594—Substitute the following for Note 3:

Janet Reno v. American Civil Liberties Union, 521 U.S. __, 117 S.Ct. 2329, 138 L.Ed.2d 874 (1997). The Supreme Court ruled that the

Internet should receive the highest level of First Amendment protection. The Court struck down two provisions of the Communications Decency Act of 1996 (CDA). The first prohibited the knowing transmission of "indecent" messages on the Internet to persons under 18; the statute did not define "indecent." The second prohibited the knowing sending or display of "patently offensive messages in a manner available to a person under 18." Such messages were defined as any communication "that, in context, depicts or describes, in terms patently offensive as measured by contemporary community standards, sexual * * * activities or organs." The Court found that the vagueness of these terms, coupled with the CDA's criminal penalties, created a severe chilling effect which, given the sweep of the statute, would affect adult speech. The Court suggested that regulation of such speech to prevent its dissemination to minors would have to rely on devices such as filtering or tagging software in order to meet a less restrictive alternative requirement. Most significantly, the Court refused to apply the looser standards for regulation that have developed for television and radio. The Court found that none of the factors justifying those standards was present on the Internet: the Internet is not invasive or likely to be accessed by accident; it is not a scarce resource; and there is no history of government regulation.

*

CHAPTER 7

SEXUALITY AND GENDER IN EDUCATION

SECTION 2

ACADEMIC FREEDOM AND ISSUES OF GENDER AND SEXUALITY

PART A. ACADEMIC FREEDOM AND SILENCING CLASSROOM DISCUSSION OF SEXUALITY

Page 625—Add the following case after the *Solmitz* Notes:

Margaret Boring v. Buncombe County Board of Educ., 136 F.3d 364 (4th Cir.1998) (*en banc*). High school teacher Margaret Boring chose the play *Independence* for students in her advanced acting class to perform in state competitions. The play depicts the dynamics of a single-parent family: the mother is divorced, one daughter is a lesbian, another is pregnant outside of marriage. After the students had won seventeen awards doing the play, the principal of the school read it and directed Boring not to perform the play again at the state competition; he later allowed the play to be performed, with deletions he suggested. The next year, the principal asked that Boring be transferred to another school; the transfer was approved by the school board, apparently based upon its view that she violated its policy against presenting "controversial materials" to students.

A panel of the Fourth Circuit, in an opinion by **Judge Motz**, reversed the trial court's dismissal of Boring's lawsuit, holding that valid First Amendment concerns were raised by the complaint. 98 F.3d 1474 (1996). Like the trial judge, Judge Motz applied the directive of *Hazelwood School Dist. v. Kuhlmeier*, 484 U.S. 260, 273 (1988), that public high schools could restrict student speech only if the restriction were "reasonably related to legitimate pedagogical concerns" (casebook, p. 607). But Judge Motz found no basis, on the face of the complaint, for deciding the issue on a motion to dismiss. The complaint's description of the play was no more provocative than the typical story from Greek mythology or the Bible.

The Fourth Circuit, sitting *en banc*, vacated the panel opinion and affirmed the district court. **Judge Widener**'s opinion for the court characterized the dispute as falling under the Supreme Court's *public employment* cases (*Pickering* [casebook, pp. 620–21] and *Connick v. Myers*, 461 U.S. 138 [1983], applied in Marjorie Rowland's case [casebook, pp. 301–04]) and not its *student speech* cases (*Fraser* and *Hazelwood*). *Connick* held that "when a public employee speaks not as a citizen upon matters of public concern, but instead as an employee upon matters of personal interest, absent the most unusual circumstances, a federal court is not the appropriate forum in which the review the wisdom of a personnel decision taken by a public agency * * *." 461 U.S. at 147. Judge Widener followed *Connick* to hold that Boring's transfer was nothing more than a personnel decision and did not implicate the First Amendment.

Moreover, the *en banc* court held, the school had a "legitimate pedagogical interest" in banning the play, because the school has "the right to fix the curriculum." See *Sweezy v. New Hampshire*, 354 U.S. 234 (1957) (leading academic freedom case). "In the case of a public school, in our opinion, it is far better public policy * * * that the makeup of the curriculum be entrusted to the local school authorities who are in some sense responsible [to the public?], rather than to the teachers, who would be responsible only to the judges, had they a First Amendment right to participate in the makeup of the curriculum." Seven judges joined this opinion.

Six judges joined the dissenting opinion of **Judge Motz**, who defended her application of *Hazelwood*, because *Connick* does not address the unique circumstances of the classroom, where the teacher engages in speech that is neither wholly private nor completely public—it is, instead, to stimulate, to enlighten, to open up discussion and impart materials. Judge Motz, further, argued that the complaint could not be dismissed under *Connick*, because depiction of an untraditional family was speech of "public concern," which *Connick* defined to be speech "relating to any matter of political, social, or other concern to the community." 461 U.S. at 146. Either Boring's presentation of an educational play was a matter of public concern (meeting *Connick*), or the *Connick* test ought not apply to educational settings.

In a separate dissent, **Judge Hamilton** objected to the *en banc* majority's characterization of the case as an "ordinary employment dispute." "Instead, as gleaned from a fair reading of the complaint, this is a case about a school principal, Fred Ivey, and a county school board * * * who targeted Margaret Boring as a scapegoat and used her to shield them from the 'heat' of the negative outcry resulting from the performance of *Independence*." He also complained that even the majority was unable to produce a single articulate *reason* for censoring the play and punishing Boring, who had followed every explicit requirement laid down by the principal and the school board. Concurring opinions by **Chief Judge Wilkinson** and **Judge Luttig** responded that if courts required reasons for curriculum decisions, judges and not parents would soon be running the school system. Judge Hamilton said this was what *Hazelwood* required. (Do you agree?)

Quaere: Does the Fourth Circuit's *en banc* opinion in *Boring* overrule the panel opinion in *Acanfora* (casebook, pp. 625–27), a pre-*Connick* decision holding that a gay teacher has a First Amendment right to come out? How, if at all, are the two cases different?

PART B. TITLE IX AND RESPONSIBILITIES OF EDUCATIONAL INSTITUTIONS TO PREVENT SEXUAL HARASSMENT

Page 639—Add the following Note after the *Nabozny* decision:

NOTE ON THE NEW TITLE IX SEXUAL HARASSMENT GUIDELINES

On March 10, 1997, the Office of Civil Rights of the Department of Education promulgated *Sexual Harassment Guidance: Harassment of Students by School Employees, Other Students, or Third Parties*, 62 Fed. Reg. 12034–50 (Mar. 13, 1997). The Guidance seeks to clarify the rules that schools receiving federal monies must follow to satisfy Title IX. As the casebook indicated, pp. 630–31, the Department of Education takes the position that both *quid pro quo* harassment (such as *Franklin*) and hostile school environment harassment (such as that Murillo complained of in *Cohen*) violate Title IX. The violative harassment can either be *sexual* or *gender-based* and can be by students or employees of the *opposite sex* or the *same sex*.

"Although Title IX does not prohibit discrimination on the basis of sexual orientation, sexual harassment directed at gay or lesbian students may constitute sexual harassment prohibited by Title IX. For example, if students heckle another student with comments based on the student's sexual orientation (e.g., 'gay students are not welcome at this table in the cafeteria'), but their actions or language do not involve sexual conduct, their actions would not be sexual harassment covered by Title IX. On the other hand, harassing conduct of a sexual nature directed toward gay or lesbian students (e.g., if a male student or a group of male students target a lesbian student for physical sexual advances) may create a sexually hostile environment and, therefore, may be prohibited by Title IX." 62 Fed. Reg. at 12039. Would *Nabozny* fall under this guidance?

If Jamie Nabozny's claim were allowable as a sex discrimination claim, he would still have to meet the Guidance's suggestions for hostile environment harassment, which is created "if conduct of a sexual nature is sufficiently severe, persistent, or pervasive to limit a student's ability to participate in or benefit from the education program or to create a hostile or abusive educational environment." *Id.* at 12041. In making a determination whether conduct is sufficiently severe or persistent or pervasive, the decisionmaker looks at the totality of the circumstances, including "the degree to which the conduct affected one or more students' education"; whether there was a "tangible obvious injury"; "the type, frequency, and duration of the conduct"; the relationship between harassers and harassee; the number of individuals involved; other incidents at the schools; and the sexual nature, if any, of the acts. "For instance, if a young woman is taunted by one or more young men about her breasts or genital area or both, OCR may find that a hostile environment has been created, particularly if the conduct has gone on for some time, takes place throughout the school, or if the taunts are made by a number of students. The more severe the conduct, the less the need to show a repetitive series of incidents * * *." *Id.*

The Guidance provides that covered educational institutions are always liable for *quid pro quo* harassment by school employees, even if the school was not aware of the sexual harassment. *Id.* at 12039. That guidance has been rejected by the Supreme Court in *Gebser v. Lago Vista Indep. Sch. Dist.*, 118 S.Ct. 1989 (1998), which construed Title IX to afford liability for teacher-student sexual harassment only if a school district official who has authority to institute corrective measures on the district's behalf has actual notice of, and is deliberately indifferent to, the sexual harassment and did nothing to correct it. Under this standard, would Alice Murillo have had a valid Title IX claim if SBVC had not taken disciplinary action against Professor Cohen? Does the Supreme Court's rejection of the Department's position as to this issue undermine the authority of its other guidances? It is hard to tell at this point, but the *Gebser* Court's reasons for not deferring to the Guidance rested upon its rejection of the Title VII analogy upon which the Education Department relied. Instead, the Court emphasized the difference between Title VII and Title IX: the former expressly gives victims a claim for relief in damages, the latter does not. Although the Supreme Court has implied a claim for relief for Title IX, the circumstances of liability should be conservatively drawn, said the Court majority in *Gebser*.

Finally, the Guidance provides that a school is liable for hostile environment harassment if "(i) a hostile environment exists in the school's programs or activities; (ii) the school knows or should have known of the harassment; and (iii) the school fails to take immediate and appropriate corrective action." *Id.* at 12039. This guidance has been most controversial of all. Consider the *Rowinsky* case in the book, pp. 639–44, and the next Note: Should schools be liable for peer harassment at all? Should Alice Murillo but not Jamie Nabozny have a Title IX claim for relief?

Page 644—Add the following Note after the *Rowinsky* decision:

NOTE ON POST-*ROWINSKY* CASELAW ON TITLE IX LIABILITY FOR PEER HARASSMENT

After Judge Smith's decision in *Rowinsky*, the Eleventh Circuit, which had found a claim for relief (casebook, p. 641), reversed course, vacating its earlier decision and following Judge Smith. *Davis v. Monroe County Bd. of Educ.*, 120 F.3d 1390 (11th Cir.1997) *(en banc)*. After the Department of Education Guidance was announced, however, one other circuit ruled that students do have a claim for relief for peer harassment if the school fails to take action once they actually knew the harassment was taking place, *Doe v. University of Illinois*, 138 F.3d 653 (7th Cir.1998) (petition for rehearing *en banc* denied). A panel of the Fourth Circuit also allowed a Title IX claim by a female college student who alleged she had been gang-raped by members of the school's football team and that the college "knew or should have known about the abuses," *Brzonkala v. VPI*, 132 F.3d 949 (4th Cir.1997), but the Fourth Circuit has vacated the panel decision and heard the case *en banc*. The recent Supreme Court decision in *Gebser* (see previous Note in this Supplement), which arose from school employee misconduct, would require *actual knowledge* at the very least for the school to be liable (contrary to Judge Cummings' majority opinion in *Doe* and consistent with Judge Coffey's concurring opinion). The Supreme Court did not resolve the *Rowinsky* issue but is obviously concerned that schools (already in apparent decline) not be deluged with lawsuits. Should *Rowinsky* be rejected in light of the Department's Guidance and the statutory language and policy? Or should the Department's Guidance be rejected on this issue, for the reasons it was rejected in *Gebser* on the *quid pro quo* liability issue?

*

CHAPTER 8

Citizenship and Community in a Sexualized World

Section 1

Accommodating Religion in a Sexualized World

Page 696—Add the following Note just before the Georgetown Case:

NOTE ON *CITY OF BOERNE v. FLORES* AND RELIGIOUS FREEDOM IN THE POST–RFRA WORLD

As the casebook noted (pp. 694–96), the Religious Freedom Restoration Act (RFRA) had shown fewer teeth than its proponents had expected, and the Supreme Court declared it unconstitutional as applied to the states in *City of Boerne v. Flores*, 117 S.Ct. 2157 (1997). RFRA had been adopted under Congress' authority to "enforce" the Fourteenth Amendment, § 5. Although several Justices continued to believe *Employment Division v. Smith*, 494 U.S. 872 (1990) wrongly decided, the Court without dissent ruled that if *Smith* were good law (as the Court majority reaffirmed) RFRA was unconstitutional, because it undermined rather than enforced the Fourteenth Amendment. With RFRA out of the picture for state regulation, the positions of Judge Bellacosa in *Ware* (casebook, pp. 692–93) and Justice Werdegar in *Smith v. FEHC* (casebook, pp. 695–96) would appear stronger. But are the RFRA concerns entirely out of the picture? Consider:

1. *Remnant of RFRA?* The reasoning of *Flores* rested upon ideas of federalism and, hence, might leave RFRA applicable to federal government actions. Maybe even to the District of Columbia, over which Congress has independent, plenary jurisdiction. If that were so, then RFRA might apply to a new version of the Georgetown Case immediately following (casebook, pp. 696–708). For an argument that RFRA may not survive even as to the federal government, see Ira Lupu, "Why the Congress Was Wrong and the Court Was Right—Reflections on *City of Boerne v. Archbishop Flores*," 39 *Wm. & Mary L. Rev.* (forthcoming 1998).

2. *RFRA Redivivus?* Congress is considering a new version of RFRA, grounded upon its Commerce Clause powers, the same authority under which Congress enacted the Civil Rights Act of 1964.[a] The problem with this course is that the Supreme Court has held that Congress cannot abrogate state Eleventh Amendment immunity under its Commerce Clause powers, *Seminole Tribe of Florida v. Florida*, 517 U.S. 44 (1996). Congress can abrogate state immunity under its Fourteenth Amendment powers, *Fitzpatrick v. Bitzer*, 427 U.S. 445 (1976), but *Flores* prevents Congress from supplanting *Smith* under those powers. What options are left to Congress? Some states, such as California and New Jersey, are actively considering their own RFRAs. If California enacted a junior RFRA, should *Smith v. FEHC* be reconsidered? (Remember that the swing vote, that of Justice Mosk, turned on his correct prediction that RFRA would be found unconstitutional.)

3. *Rethinking Free Exercise.* The Supreme Court's opinion in *Smith v. Employment Division* distinguished *Yoder* on the ground that it involved not just free exercise rights, but also parental privacy rights of a constitutional dimension. One doctrinal way to defend Chief Judge Kaye's sensitivity to religious claims in *Ware* is to view the case as involving both free exercise and privacy elements; such a reading might also support the dissenters' views in Evelyn Smith's case, if you think her complaint implicates the constitutional freedom of association such as that explored in Chapter 5, § 1 (the Jaycees and Boston Parade Cases). Perhaps academic freedom could play that role in the Georgetown Case that follows.

Page 713—Add the following Note right after the Cover excerpt:

NOTE ON *NOMOS* AND FREE EXERCISE JURISPRUDENCE

Deploy Cover's theory to revisit the free exercise issues in the Cases of the Brethren (*Ware*), the Presbyterian Landlord (*Evelyn Smith*), and

---

a. See *Protecting Religious Freedom After* Boerne v. Flores: *Hearing Before the Subcomm. on the Constitution of the House* *Comm. on the Judiciary*, 104th Cong., 1st Sess. (July 14, 1997).

Georgetown University. One of us has combined Cover's theory of nomic communities with the insights of feminist and gaylegal jurisprudence to argue for a precept of statutory interpretation: Courts should interpret broadly written antidiscrimination statutes to accommodate religious free exercise and other nomic associational concerns. This is what Chief Judge Kaye did in *Ware* and Judge Mack did in *Georgetown*.[b] It is what the Massachusetts courts should have done in *Hurley* (casebook, pp. 438–41). Justice Kennard, one of the dissenters in *Evelyn Smith*, relied on our theory to construe California's public accommodation law not to apply to the Boy Scouts (*Curran*, Chapter 5 of this Supplement, pp. 63–64). This is beyond the religious contexts emphasized by Professor Cover but within the spirit of our article. Should the nomic idea be extended that far? Is *Dale v. Boy Scouts of America* (Supplement, pp. 58–63), wrongly decided?

More generally, the idea of nomic diversity would support a rule of statutory or even constitutional interpretation that would exempt religious seminaries and other "core" institutions from nondiscrimination laws where religious principle requires discrimination on the basis of sexual orientation, sex, or even race. (Note that ENDA [casebook, appendix 4] has a broad exemption, as do almost all other nondiscrimination laws.) Is this going too far?

b. See William Eskridge, Jr., "A Jurisprudence of 'Coming Out': Religion, Homosexuality, and Collisions of Liberty and Equality in American Public Law," 106 *Yale L.J.* 2411 (1997).

CITIZENS IN CONFLICT: ANTI–CIVIL RIGHTS AND ANTI–GAY INITIATIVES

PART C. THE CONSTITUTIONALITY OF ANTI–GAY INITIATIVES

Page 733—Add the following decision after *Romer v. Evans* and before Problem 8–3:

Equality Foundation of Greater Cincinnati, et al. v. City of Cincinnati, et al.

United States Court of Appeals for the Sixth Circuit, 1997.
128 F.3d 289, *rehearing en banc denied*, 1998 WL 101701 (1998).

[This decision is reprinted in Chapter 1, § 3 of this Supplement, pp. 9–12. Is it properly distinguishable from Colorado's Amendment 2?]

Page 733—Add the following to Problem 8–3:

Unlike the initiatives involved in the Riverside, Colorado, and Cincinnati cases, most antigay initiatives and referenda—both before and after *Romer v. Evans*—have been targeted rather than sweeping. In January 1998, for example, voters in Maine narrowly voted to repeal a statewide gay rights law the legislature had passed in 1997. In November 1998, voters in Alaska and Hawaii will decide on state constitutional amendments relating to same-sex marriage. The proposed Alaska amendment would read it out of the state constitution entirely, while the proposed Hawaii amendment would authorize the legislature to do the same thing; the stories and texts of the amendments can be found in a Note to Chapter 9, § 2 of this Supplement, pp. 111–12.

Quaere: Should more targeted antigay initiatives be skeptically scrutinized under equal protection review? More seriously than similar measures adopted by the legislature? Consider the following Note.

NOTE ON HEIGHTENED JUDICIAL REVIEW OF POPULAR INITIATIVES AND REFERENDA

Most scholars have urged the U.S. Supreme Court and state high courts to scrutinize popular initiatives more carefully for equal protection violations than the Court gives to ordinary legislation.[c] *Evans* might be read to sympathize with this academic perspective. If so, it and the other cases are vulnerable to the argument from democracy: courts should be more rather than less reluctant to overturn legislation when it is clearly responsive to majority preferences. In light of this objection, should such initiatives be scrutinized more exactingly?

The main argument for heightened review is that the Constitution adopts a "republican" structure rather than direct democracy (see *Federalist* No. 10) for the national government and expresses a preference for the same at the state level (U.S. Const. Art. IV). The reason for the Constitution's policy is the greater preference for the status quo and deliberation assured by republican governance. Before a bill becomes law, it must pass through two legislative chambers and a possible executive veto. This assures more opportunities for affected minorities to block or ameliorate the harm to them from representative than popular legislation. Possibilities for distortion and emotional appeals are more likely in direct democracy, where voters are often confused by the phrasing of initiatives and demagogued by professional politicians or grass-roots organizers. Also, because voting is open and public in the representative but not initiative process, critics of direct democracy fear that prejudice will be more readily expressed in the latter than the former.

Other scholars reject or caution against this academic conventional wisdom.[d] Initiatives are an intrinsically fair way for the voting population to focus on an issue that concerns them, and are often a better path to active citizen engagement in substantive issues. Public choice theory, for example, suggests that legislators have incentives not to confront or resolve conflictual issues, and this may have been the reason the Colorado legislature ducked the issue of sexual orientation protections at the local level. Moreover, the same kinds of questions raised against direct democracy— the inability of minorities to win, the lack of genuine deliberation, private interests winning over the common good—have been posed by public choice theorists criticizing representative democracy. Lynn Baker criticizes Derrick Bell and Julian Eule, the two main critics of direct democracy, for employing "an interest group or pluralist model of lawmaking by ordinary citizens, but a republican or public-interest model of lawmaking by legislatures" (Baker, p. 751).

c.   E.g., Derrick Bell, Jr., "The Referendum: Democracy's Barrier to Racial Equality," 54 *Wash. L. Rev.* 1 (1978); Julian Eule, "Judicial Review of Direct Democracy," 99 *Yale L.J.* 1503 (1990); Daniel Lowenstein, "California Initiatives and the Single–Subject Rule," 30 *UCLA L. Rev.* 936 (1983) (state constitutional review); Lawrence Sager, "Insular Majorities Unabated," 91 *Harv. L. Rev.* 1373 (1978).

d.   See Lynn Baker, "Direct Democracy and Discrimination: A Public Choice Perspective," 67 *Chi-Kent L. Rev.* 707 (1992); Richard Briffault, "Distrust of Democracy," 63 *Tex. L. Rev.* 1347 (1985) (book review); Clayton Gillette, "Plebscites, Participation, and Collective Action in Local Government Law," 86 *Mich. L. Rev.* 930 (1988).

How does the Colorado experience bear on these arguments? Judge Hans Linde argues that the history of antigay initiatives supports the conventional academic wisdom and heightened judicial review under Article IV.[e] As soon as states and municipalities stopped witch-hunting lesbian and gay employees and couples and starting granting these citizens equal rights, antigay initiatives sought to overturn positive laws, by appeals to arguments that gay people are predatory child molesters (the main argument in the 1970s) or that the community should not "promote the homosexual lifestyle" by providing "special rights" (the main argument in the 1990s). Barbara Gamble, "Putting Civil Rights to Popular Vote," 41 *Am.J. Pol. Sci.* 245 (1997), found that although only one-third of all ballot measures pass (on average), voters approved 30 of the 38 measures restricting gay rights that she was able to identify for the period 1959–1993.

See Jane Schacter, "The Pursuit of 'Popular Intent': 'Interpretive Dilemmas in Direct Democracy,' " 105 *Yale L.J.* 107 (1995), for a thorough introduction to judicial construction of initiatives creating or amending state statutes.

Page 738—Add the following materials at the end of the Note on the Schacter article:

Consider Schacter's thesis and the Kennedy–Scalia debate in *Romer v. Evans* in light of the ballot materials provided to voters by the sponsors of Colorado Amendment 2. We first saw them appended to an article by Professor Robert Nagel, and he referred us to Colorado For Family Values, which graciously provided us with originals and permission to reprint their pamphlet, which occupies the immediately following pages of this Supplement. We have not edited the pamphlet in any way.

---

e. See Hans Linde, "When Is Initiative Lawmaking Not 'Republican Government'?," 17 *Hast. Conts'l L.Q.* 159 (1989). On the intellectual history of antigay initiatives, see William Eskridge, Jr., "Challenging the Apartheid of the Closet, 1961–1981," 25 *Hofstra L. Rev.* 817, 928–30 (1997).

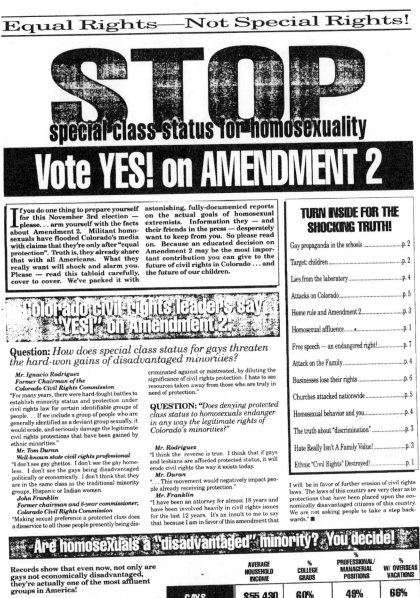

Equal Rights—Not Special Rights!

STOP special class status for homosexuality

Vote YES! on AMENDMENT 2

If you do one thing to prepare yourself for this November 3rd election — please. . . arm yourself with the facts about Amendment 2. Militant homosexuals have flooded Colorado's media with claims that they're only after "equal protection". Truth is, they already share that with all Americans. What they really want will shock and alarm you. Please — read this tabloid carefully, cover to cover. We've packed it with astonishing, fully-documented reports on the actual goals of homosexual extremists. Information they — and their friends in the press — desperately want to keep from you. So please read on. Because an educated decision on Amendment 2 may be the most important contribution you can give to the future of civil rights in Colorado . . . and the future of our children.

Colorado civil rights leaders say "YES!" on Amendment 2

Question: *How does special class status for gays threaten the hard-won gains of disadvantaged minorities?*

Mr. Ignacio Rodriguez
Former Chairman of the
Colorado Civil Rights Commission
"For many years, there were hard-fought battles to establish minority status and protection under civil rights law for certain identifiable groups of people. . . If we include a group of people who are generally identified as a deviant group sexually, it would erode, and seriously damage the legitimate civil rights protections that have been gained by ethnic minorities."

Mr. Tom Duran
Well-known state civil rights professional
"I don't see gay ghettos. I don't see the gay homeless. I don't see the gays being disadvantaged politically or economically. I don't think that they are in the same class as the traditional minority groups, Hispanic or Indian women.

John Franklin
Former chairman and 8-year commissioner,
Colorado Civil Rights Commission
"Making sexual preference a protected class does a disservice to all those people presently being discriminated against or mistreated, by diluting the significance of civil rights protection. I hate to see resources taken away from those who are truly in need of protection."

QUESTION: *"Does denying protected class status to homosexuals endanger in any way the legitimate rights of Colorado's minorities?"*

Mr. Rodriguez
"I think the reverse is true. I think that if gays and lesbians are afforded protected status, it will erode civil rights the way it exists today.

Mr. Duran
". . . This movement would negatively impact people already receiving protection."

Mr. Franklin
"I have been an attorney for almost 18 years and have been involved heavily in civil rights issues for the last 12 years. It's an insult to me to say that because I am in favor of this amendment that I will be in favor of further erosion of civil rights laws. The laws of this country are very clear as to protections that have been placed upon the economically disadvantaged citizens of this country. We are not asking people to take a step backwards." ■

Are homosexuals a "disadvantaged" minority? You decide!

Records show that even now, not only are gays not economically disadvantaged, they're actually one of the most affluent groups in America!

✔ On July 18, 1991, the Wall Street Journal reported the results of a nation-wide marketing survey about gay income levels. The survey reported that gays' average income was more than $30,000 over that of the average Americans'. Gays were over three times more likely to be college graduates. Three times more likely to hold professional or managerial positions. Four times more likely to be overseas travelers. These are people with tons of discretionary income!

please turn to page 2

	AVERAGE HOUSEHOLD INCOME	% COLLEGE GRADS	% PROFESSIONAL/ MANAGERIAL POSITIONS	% W/ OVERSEAS VACATIONS
GAYS	$55,430	60%	49%	66%
NAT'L AVERAGE	$32,286	18%	16%	14%
DISADVANTAGED AFR. AMERICANS	$12,166	less than 5%	less than 1%	less than 1%

VOTE YES ON AMENDMENT 2

EQUAL RIGHTS—NOT SPECIAL RIGHTS!

Sound like an oppressed minority to you? Judge for yourself — Take a look at the hardships Black Americans have had to face. Then see if homosexuals compare. Special rights for homosexuals just isn't fair — especially to disadvantaged minorities in Colorado. Please vote YES! on Amendment 2.

HISTORICALLY ACCEPTED EVIDENCES OF DISCRIMINATION	BLACK AMERICANS	HOMOSEXUALS
Ever denied the right to vote?	Yes	No
Ever faced legal segregation?	Yes	No
Ever denied access by law to public drinking fountains, restrooms	Yes	No
Ever denied access by law to businesses, restaurants, barber shops, etc.?	Yes	No
Evidence of systematic discrimination in housing and jobs in Colorado today?	Yes	No
Verifiable economic hardship as a result of discrimination? (see page 3)	Yes	No

TARGET: CHILDREN

Lately, America's been hearing alot about the subject of childhood sexual abuse. This terrible epidemic has scarred countless young lives and destroyed thousands of families. But what militant homosexuals don't want you to know is the large role they play in this epidemic. In fact, pedophilia (the sexual molestation of children) is actually an accepted part of the homosexual community!

✔ David Thorstad, founding member of the gay organization called the North American Man-Boy Love Association, a group whose motto is "Sex by eight, or it's too late" and a former president of the Gay Activist Alliance of New York, writes:

"The issue of man-boy love has intersected the gay movement since the late nineteenth century." Thorstad complains that pedophilia is being swept under the rug by the gay-rights movement, which "... seeks to sanitize the image of homosexuality to facilitate its entrance into the social mainstream."

"Man-Boy Love and the American Gay Movement" from The Journal of Homosexuality, 20, 1990, pp. 251-252).

✔ Two homosexual researchers writing in *The Gay Report* reported that 73% of homosexuals surveyed had at some time had sex with boys sixteen to nineteen years of age or younger!

✔ The British Journal of Sexual Medicine (April 1987) published a study in which homosexuals are statistically about 18 times more likely to engage in sex with minors than heterosexuals.

The North American Man-Boy Love Association, an accepted member of the homosexual community, proudly waves its motto at gay-pride parades: *"Sex by Eight, or It's Too Late"*. And they're dedicated to repealing age-of-consent laws!

✔ *Psychological Reports* (1986, #58, pp. 327-337) published a report revealing that homosexuals, who represent perhaps 2% of the population, perpetrate more than one-third of all reported child molestations!

✔ The 1972 Gay Rights Platform, which has not changed or been rescinded in twenty years, calls for (1) "Repeal of all state laws prohibiting private sexual acts involving consenting persons" [not consenting adults] and (2) "Repeal of all laws governing the age of sexual consent."

Don't let gay militant double-talk hide their true intentions. Sexual molestation of children is a large part of many homosexuals' lifestyle — part of the very lifestyle "gay-rights" activists want government to give special class, ethnic status! Say no to sexual perversion with children — **vote YES! on Amendment 2!** ■

Homosexual indoctrination in the schools? IT'S HAPPENING IN COLORADO!

Here's a frightening example of the "gay-rights" agenda right here in our state: a 1992 Denver Public Schools Health and Science Education teachers' guide entitled "Gay and Lesbian Youth Tools for Educators", presented to teachers by gay instructors during a taxpayer-funded continuing education course. This guide contains a questionnaire designed to be answered by heterosexual junior high and high school students. It asks, among others, these questions:

3. *Is it possible your heterosexuality is just a phase you may outgrow?*

5. *Is it possible that all you need is a good gay lover?*

7. *If you have never slept with a person of the same sex, how do you know that you would not prefer to do so?*

14. *How can you hope to become a whole person if you limit yourself to an exclusive heterosexual object choice and remain unwilling to explore and develop your normal, natural, healthy homosexual potential?*

And the brochure goes on — aggressively promoting acceptance of homosexuality, bisexuality, lesbianism, and condom use, complete with graphic, "how-to" descriptions. It also suggests that teachers distribute to children pamphlets containing phone numbers of possible adult gay mentors, who may encourage children to experiment with gay behavior. Imagine your tax money being spent to try and convince children — maybe even your own — that they should consider homosexuality! In the public schools! This is the true, sinister face of "gay-rights". Please — vote **"YES" on Amendment 2,** or you may be denied the chance to protest outrages like this one! ■

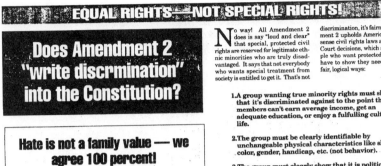

EQUAL RIGHTS — NOT SPECIAL RIGHTS!

Does Amendment 2 "write discrmination" into the Constitution?

Hate is not a family value — we agree 100 percent!

Opponents of Amendment 2 have been plastering the state with posters saying that "Hate Is Not A Family Value". But Colorado for Family Values, sponsor of Amendment 2, agree with that statement 100 percent! That's exactly why we've filled this tabloid with "just the facts"; because facts don't hate, they just are.

We agree that Hate Is Not A Family Value so much, nearly a year ago we announced and implemented the statewide "No Room for Hatred" campaign, to let every Coloradan know loud and clear that there's no room on either side of this debate for hatred of any kind.

Unfortunately, our opponents didn't get the message. Although we invited them to join us in sending a strong, unified no-hatred statement to the people of Colorado, after one letter suggesting an interest, they continuously refused to respond to our repeated attempts to follow through. Obviously, coming out against hatred wasn't on their agenda back then:

✔ Soon after that, crude, obviously forged "hate" literature supposedly written by us, started being circulated by our opponents.

✔ Militant gays started shouting obscenities at CFV meetings.

✔ Men in drag started showing up outside our meetings, soliciting money in CFV's name.

✔ Sabotage and threatening posters started becoming daily occurences at our headquarters.

✔ One EPOC leader repeated her frequently-expressed hope that we all "rot in hell" and threatened, "we're gonna get you [expletive deleted]'s."

Colorado for Family Values, on the other hand, made "No Room for Hatred" a cornerstone of our successful and completely peaceful, petition drive:

✔ We've declined to attend rallies where the chance of unpleasantness existed.

✔ We encouraged gay-rights opponents to stay away from so-called "pride" parades to ensure that the peace was kept.

✔ We published a Resolution In Support of Principled Debate, which EPOC received and ignored.

✔ We've stuck to the facts. We've delivered on our promise to make our case logically and honestly to the people of Colorado. And we continue today. We've filled this tabloid with facts about the militant gay agenda not to make you hate them, but to warn you about the danger their goals represent to you and your children's rights. As proof that the gay lifestyle has nothing in common with the kinds of traits and behaviors America has protected in its civil rights laws. And as proof that it isn't the kind of behavior society needs to reward with special class status. So please — if you stand with us against hatred toward any fellow Coloradans — **vote YES! November 3rd on Amendment 2.** ■

No way! All Amendment 2 does is say "loud and clear" that special, protected civil rights are reserved for legitimate ethnic minorities who are truly disadvantaged. It says that not everybody who wants special treatment from society is entitled to get it. That's not discrimination, it's fairness. Amendment 2 upholds America's common-sense civil rights laws and Supreme Court decisions, which say that people who want protected class status have to show they need it, in three fair, logical ways:

1.A group wanting true minority rights must show that it's discriminated against to the point that its members can't earn average income, get an adequate education, or enjoy a fulfilling cultural life.

2.The group must be clearly identifiable by unchangeable physical characteristics like skin color, gender, handicap, etc. (not behavior).

3.The group must clearly show that it is politically powerless.

As you can clearly see, gays flunk all three requirements! And no group that fails to meet these requirements is entitled to make discrimination claims. These requirements are the heart and soul of civil rights protections. African/Americans, Hispanics, women, etc. all met them. For gays to get minority status, we'd have to throw these requirements out, and that would mean rewriting the whole book on civil rights!

Please, don't turn the tables on the whole history of civil rights in this country. Homosexuals deserve human rights — not special rights. **Vote YES! on Amendment 2.** ■

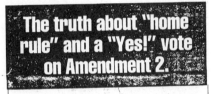

The truth about "home rule" and a "Yes!" vote on Amendment 2.

Home rule" has always been an important, legitimate part of how Coloradans govern themselves. But lately, militant gays have been crying that Amendment 2 would violate this important concept. They want you to believe that voting "Yes" on Amendment 2 means no one will ever be able to vote on a local issue again.

That's ridiculous. Here's a little truth about Amendment 2 and the home rule issue:

✔ Everyone knows some issues are "home rule" in nature, and some aren't. It's common sense: some are local in scope, others are statewide or national. If the people had no right to vote their conscience on a statewide or national level, then why would we have a State Legislature or a U.S. Congress?

✔ The hateful "Jim Crow" laws that once oppressed African/Americans in the South were "home rule" laws — enacted locally, by racist city and county officials, to keep people of color "in their place". Thankfully, the Civil Rights Act of 1964 said "No" to "Jim Crow" laws and declared loud and clear that civil rights aren't a local, "home rule" issue. They're for a whole state, even a whole nation, to decide on. Should local authorities regain complete control over civil rights?

✔ Militant homosexuals don't care a hoot for "home rule". They've been lobbying the U.S. Congress, the Courts and the Colorado Legislature on their agenda for years. Do those sound like local, "home rule" institutions to you? Of course not. When they lobbied the U.S. Congress for a national "gay-rights" law, do you think gay extremists planned to give every town in America a choice on whether to go along? Of course not. "Home rule" is a red herring, meant to confuse the issue. They've ignored "home rule" themselves for years.

✔ Gay extremists actually want you to believe there's something undemocratic, unrepresentative about YOU having a vote on this issue! What's more democratic than gathering petition signatures, then giving Coloradans a voice at the ballot box?

Amendment 2 does give everyone the right to vote their conscience about "gay-rights". That's what we'll all do on November 3rd. And if a "gay-rights" supporter tries to tell you "home rule" should prevail, just ask them this question: "Should a town in Colorado have the right to vote 'Jim Crow' laws back into existence again if they want?" We think you'll agree that that's a terrible idea. ■

In Laguna Beach, California, a city with one of the country's largest gay communities and strongest "gay-rights" ordinances, a three-year old boy entered a public park restroom. What he saw there traumatized him severely. Three grown gay men were engaging in group sex, right there in the bathroom. When he ran out to his mother, crying and upset, she attempted to file a complaint with the Laguna Beach Police Department. Their reply: with a "gay-rights" ordinance in place, there was nothing they could do. You can stop this from happening in Colorado with your "YES" vote on Amendment 2.

VOTE YES! ON AMENDMENT 2

3

EQUAL RIGHTS——NOT SPECIAL RIGHTS!

Homosexual behavior — should government protect *this*?

Militant gays want government to give their lifestyle special class status — but we think it's important to know just what kind of lifestyle they want your tax dollars to endorse. You may already know that the sexual practices of gays differ drastically from those of most of Colorado's population. But how much those practices differ — and the dangerous perversions they involve — may shock you!

✔ Let's start with number of sexual partners. 1982 U.S. Centers for Disease Control figures put the lifetime total for typical homosexuals interviewed at 500. AIDS sufferers individually studied: 1,100. In a Kinsey Institute survey, 43% of white male homosexuals estimated 500 or more, 75% 100 or more, 28% over 1,000. 79% said over half of their partners were strangers. A survey by two homosexual researchers reports 38% of lesbians having between 11 and over 300 lifetime partners.

✔ "Monogamy" is virtually unknown in the gay lifestyle. One university-published study shows that 3% of homosexuals have had fewer than 10 lifetime partners. Only 2% could be classified as either monogamous or semi-monogamous (although "monogamy" in gay terms is hardly permanent — lasting anywhere between 9 to 60 months).

✔ Gays' have been unwilling (or unable) to curb their voracious, unsafe sex practices in the face of AIDS. A 1985 study of 655 San Francisco gay men in the *American Journal of Public Health* reported that "knowledge of health guidelines was quite high, but this knowledge had no relation to sexual behavior." 59% had been unprotected, passive recipients of anal intercourse in the month before the survey. The Washington Post (June 1990) and Time Magazine (July 1990) both report that despite the threat of AIDS, gays have not restrained themselves. The Journal reported last October a study in which 45% of gay men remained sexually active after learning that they were HIV+, and incredibly, 52% of them *did not inform their partners!*

✔ Overall, surveys show that 90% of gay men engage in anal intercourse — the most high-risk sexual behavior in society today. (No wonder 83% of Colorado AIDS cases have occurred in gay males — it's a tragedy, but it's true.) About 80% of gay men surveyed have engaged in oral sex upon the anus of partners. Well over a third of gays in 1977 admitted to "fisting". In the largest study of gay men ever conducted, 29% admitted participating in "golden showers".

✔ Gays live shorter lives. In a survey of 6,211 obituaries from gay journals compared to obituaries from regular newspapers, gays who did not die of AIDS had a median age of death of 42 years old! (And 39 if AIDS was the cause.) The lesbians surveyed had a median age of death of 45.

Is this the kind of lifestyle we want to reward with special protection, and protected ethnic status? Gay activists want you to think they're "just like you" — but these statistics point out how false that is. So please remember — gays deserve, and have, human rights. But there's no way this lifestyle deserves special rights. Please **vote YES! on Amendment 2.** ■

OBJECTIVE: DESTROY THE FAMILY

If you value the role of family in the fabric of Colorado, then you have reason to fear the true agenda of "gay-rights" militants. To this angry, alienated minority, the family is the symbol of everything they attack. Consider these facts:

✔ The 1972 Gay Rights Platform called for "... Repeal of all laws governing the age of consent... of all legislative provisions that restrict the sex or number of persons entering into a marriage unit; and the extension of legal benefits to all persons who cohabit regardless of sex or numbers."

✔ Manifestoes in prominent gay-authored books (The Gay Militants, The Gay Crusaders and Out of the Closets) demand: "That all organized religions be condemned for helping in the genocide of homosexuals... That the family as we now know it be abolished... That children be placed in communal areas away from their parents, with boys and girls reared the same and cared for by adults who are under the direction of lesbian women."

✔ Gay activist Michael Swift writes "[The family unit] is a spawning ground of lies, betrayal, mediocrity, hypocrisy and violence — and will be abolished."

So if you value the family, show the militant "anti-family" activists that you stand for its protection. Your "YES" vote on Amendment 2 will keep the anti-family onslaught from getting official government approval in Colorado. ■

"We shall sodomize your sons, emblems of your feeble masculinity, of your shallow dreams and vulgar lies. We shall seduce them in your schools, in your dormitories, in your gymnasiums, in your locker rooms, in your sports arenas, in your seminaries, in your youth groups...

...The family unit — which only dampens imaginations and curbs free will, must be eliminated.

... All churches who condemn us will be closed. Our only gods are handsome young men."

— *Michael Swift, "Gay Revolutionary" writing in Gay Community News*

Don't let this kind of hatred prevail in Colorado. Tell this angry minority they deserve equal rights — but not special rights. Vote "YES!" on Amendment 2 this November 3rd.

Don't believe lies from the laboratory

Homosexuality isn't something you "are", it's something you "do".

Are gays born, or made? It's a question on a lot of people's minds. And militant gays, in order to strengthen their demand for special class status, are desperate to *manufacture* evidence that homosexuality is a genetic condition. Their strategy: flood the media with reports of so-called "discoveries", knowing full-well the average person isn't trained in telling true scientific evidence from false.

So first, here are some conclusions from impartial, neutral scientists:

✔ "Homosexuality is not innate... there is no inevitable genetically inborn propensity toward the choice of a partner of either the same or opposite sex" (Socarides, C.W., "Homosexuality: Basic Concepts and Psychodynamics," *International Journal of Psychiatry*, Vol. 10 [March 1972, p. 118].

✔ "The genetic theory of homosexuality has been generally discarded today... no serious scientist today suggests that a simple cause-effect relationship applies" (Masters, Johnson and Kolodny, *Human Sexuality*, Boston: Little, Brown & Co., 1984, p. 319).

✔ "We're born man, woman and sexual beings. We learn our sexual preferences and orientations"(Masters and Johnson, interview, UPI, April 23, 1979.)

✔ "There is little evidence of the existence of such a thing as innate perversity..." (Alfred Kinsey, as reported by W.B. Pomeroy, Dr. Kinsey and the Institute for Sex Research, New York: Harper & Row, 1972, p. 273.)

So what about the so-called "gay brains" study? Or the "gay twins" study — both of which got so much widespread, unquestioning media coverage? The "gay brain" study, which claimed to find a difference in brain chemistry between the corpses of gays and heterosexuals...

✔ ... ignored the fact that the brain cells in question have never been proven to actually work together in any way whatsoever!

✔ ... as a gay writer himself pointed out, "It turns out that LeVay doesn't know anything about the sexual orientation of his control group, the 16 corpses 'presumed heterosexual.' A sloppy control like this is... enough by itself to invalidate the study." (Michael Botkin, Salk and Pepper, Bay Area Reporter, September 5, 1991, pp. 21-24)

✔ ... most important of all: do these supposed differences point to a *cause* or a *result* of homosexuality? "Scientist" LeVay, an avowed homosexual who has now become a gay activist himself, answered, on national television: "I can't say. But I'll bet the house that it's the cause." How's that for scientific fairness?

✔ ...the "gay twins" study, which claims to show that identical twins are more likely to both become homosexual, ignores the fact that identical twins share their environments even more closely than other twins, and actually recruited its subjects from gay magazines! More damaging still, when the study's subjects actually spoke for themselves, there was no difference between fraternal twins and adopted brothers!

We could go on, but you get the point: these "scientific studies" are nothing more than political propaganda, laboratory-style — "research" twisted to fit a pre-arranged conclusion. Don't let fake science fool you — being gay isn't like being born Black or Hispanic, or a Woman, or even being physically disabled. That's yet another reason why they don't deserve protected class status! Please — to safeguard civil rights for the truly disadvantaged, **vote YES! on Amendment 2** ■

VOTE YES! ON AMENDMENT 2

EQUAL RIGHTS—NOT SPECIAL RIGHTS!

"Gay-rights" destroys basic freedoms!

Ann Lockwood should have known better. Assuming that freedom of association was still allowed in Madison, Wisconsin, Ann put a notice in the classifieds for a second roommate.

But Ann didn't count on Madison's "gay-rights" ordinance. When an open lesbian answered Ann's ad and was politely declined by Ann and her heterosexual roommate, the lesbian filed a complaint. And "gay rights" suddenly showed their true colors.

Ann and her roommate were:

✔ summoned before a "fact-finding" board

✔ interrogated for hours

✔ assessed fines totalling $1500

✔ assigned to "sensitivity" classes, taught by lesbians, designed to realign their "politically incorrect" views on homosexuality.

Ann pleaded that the fines would bankrupt her. "That's not our problem," she was told.

✔ Finally, both were ordered to report periodically to the city for monitoring of their lifestyle — for the next three years.

But this isn't just some exceptional, "one-in-a-million" tale of justice betrayed:

✔ In Minnesota, the Catholic Archdiocese was assessed $35,000 in fines and damages for refusing to open Church facilities to a homosexual club.

✔ In Hawaii, churches have been warned that regardless of their beliefs, all staff positions save the pastorate must be made available to homosexuals.

✔ Again in Minnesota, a Catholic priest was sued, in a case that dragged on for years, simply for refusing to hire a homosexual to teach in a Catholic school!

✔ A 1992 "gay-rights" statute in New Jersey prohibits employers from discriminating on the basis of sexual orientation in hiring and firing. The same law could force churches to unite homosexuals in marriage.

✔ In Minneapolis, Big Brothers was prosecuted for merely telling one mother that a prospective Big Brother was homosexual. After years of legal harassment, Big Brothers has adopted a national policy of "accepting gay men as prospective Big Brothers to fatherless youths."

✔ Constitutional attorneys estimate the cost of fighting charges filed under "gay-rights" legislation to a Supreme Court decision as nearly $250,000.

It goes on and on. Cut through the gushy slogans about "tolerance" and "freedom" militant gays cloak themselves in, and you discover actions saying exactly the opposite. Actions revealing a concerted attack on the right of any American to hold, speak or live out non–"politically correct" beliefs.

Amendment 2 will safeguard your right to disagree with the militant gay mindset. Please — vote "YES" on 2 November 3rd. ∎

Churches attacked nationwide!

In the related article "Gay-rights destroys basic freedoms" we tell you how churches in "gay-rights" cities and states are being forced to violate their beliefs in their hiring practices, or face legal retaliation. But in many places, churches are actually being physically attacked by militant gays, services invaded, clergy assaulted. Here's just a few instances of this unreported outrage:

✔ New York's St. Patrick's Cathedral was attacked in 1989 by extremists from ACT-UP!, the gay shock-troop organization. The chanting and shouting homosexuals paraded down the aisles of the Cathedral, incensed at Cardinal John O'Connor's stand against homosexuality. They pelted the congregation with condoms, and defiled the communion elements, completely bringing the Mass to a halt before having to be forcibly removed from the service.

✔ In Costa Mesa, California, militant gays angry at Calvary Chapel's ministry outreach to the Orange County gay community invaded that church during Sunday morning services. The church that launched the "Jesus People" movement of the sixties had its aisles filled with gays shouting and fondling themselves in full view of families in the congregation. Attempts to remove them nearly resulted in serious violence.

✔ On Saturday, November 16, 1991, a group of AIDS demonstrators dressed in suits and ties infiltrated a Family Concerns Conference at the First Baptist Church of Atlanta, then peppered the diners with hundreds of condoms, all the while chanting, "safer sex saves lives."

If "gay-rights" succeed and homosexuals gain protected class status, this kind of abuse will continue, even increase. Protect your right to worship and believe as you choose — vote "YES" on Amendment 2. ∎

Gay-rights abuses here in Colorado!

Already, here in our state, various "gay-rights" ordinances and policies are violating the rights of our citizens. Please read for the untold story:

✔ Last year's statewide proposed "Ethnic Harassment Bill" would have made it a hate crime for any Colorado citizen to speak negatively about homosexuality. A pastor or member of the clergy could have faced felony charges for saying what he/she believes!

Thankfully, this outrage was defeated in committee.

✔ This year, the Student Association of Metro State College ordered all campus religious groups to admit homosexuals or face expulsion. Menorah Ministries, a small Christian organization on campus, became the target of an intimidation campaign merely because, in accordance with its beliefs, it declined to admit homosexual members.

✔ Already in Boulder, apartment dwellers and dorm-residing students alike are being told they are legally prohibited from asking if a prospective roommate is gay. Furthermore, if they've been lied to and want to change roommates, the financial burden is on them!

Imagine being the parent of a CU/Boulder student: your child is uncomfortable with the thought of living with a homosexual, but is prohibited from learning about the lifestyle of his/her roommate. Three months into the term, the roommate "comes out" and begins living an active gay lifestyle, in close quarters with your child. What can you or your child do about it? According to the "law" in Boulder, nothing — unless you want to undergo the severe inconvenience and thousands of dollars in expenses involved in changing roommates mid-semester, and launching into the difficult search for a new one.

Whether you're a student or an apartment resident, the result is the same. You can ask a prospective roommate any question you want, but if you ask "Are you gay?", you face charges from the city. If you decide to change roommates, you face thousands of dollars in expenses.

Don't let these abuses of civil rights come to your town — vote "YES" on Amendment 2 and protect your freedom of conscience! ∎

DAY-CARE CENTER

RESUME

I'M SORRY SIR. YOUR CREDENTIALS ARE PERFECT--BUT WE HAVEN'T FILLED OUR QUOTA OF HOMOSEXUALS!

VOTE YES! ON AMENDMENT 2!

EQUAL RIGHTS — NOT SPECIAL RIGHTS!

Under "gay-rights", free-speech becomes an endangered species!

✔ You probably remember the orchestrated attack that gay militants and their supporters hurled on Coach McCartney this year for speaking his mind. Simply for stating his beliefs, in response to reporters' constant questions, he was subjected to a wave of media and pro gay-rights abuse. It was as if the First Amendment has suddenly been suspended in the state of Colorado! But don't think that was an isolated occurence:

✔ Last year, an ethnic harassment bill (which was thankfully defeated in committee) would have made it a felony hate crime to speak negatively about homosexuality! Even a member of the clergy could have faced criminal penalties for preaching against the homosexual lifestyle. Yes, it can happen in America.

✔ Several public figures who have made known their support for Amendment 2 have received specific, serious death threats. Others have been threatened in their careers. Some have been forced to move from offices or homes. Others have had to hire extra security — all because they spoke in favor of Amendment 2.

Don't let this attack on the free-speech rights of all Coloradans succeed! Stand up for freedom of speech by voting "YES!" on Amendment 2. ∎

Amendment 2 doesn't hinge on religion or morality. And it *certainly* isn't about hatred.

It's about fairness.

What's fair about an affluent group gaining minority privileges simply for what they do in bed? What's fair about making some one's opinion illegal just because it isn't "politically correct"? What's fair about people who enjoy all the rights and privileges of American citizenship asking for special status — just because they're unhappy with the rights they already have?

Nothing, we say. If you agree with us, we ask you to please Vote "Yes" on Amendment 2 in November! ∎

Businesses: one more burden to bear

If you own or manage a business, you already know how many rules and regulations make your job so difficult already. But "gay-rights" adds another substantial layer of liability and responsibility in favor of a group that already enjoys substantial income and professional privileges! Consider just a few of the burdens you'll face under "gay-rights":

✔ How do you know if a job applicant is "gay"? Does saying so make it a fact? What would keep a would-be employee from claiming to be homosexual in order to gain an advantage over other applicants?

✔ Under state or municipal ordinances, an employer charged with discrimination pays not only for his own defense, but, through taxation, for its own prosecution. Even if you win, you can still face exorbitant attorney's fees.

✔ Will homosexual employees — who are now starting to think of themselves as a brand-new "gender", demand their own separate bathrooms? How will you afford to build them if the demand is made — backed up by law?

✔ Will you be hampered in potential disciplinary actions when a homosexual employee harasses or propositions others around him/her? If they claim the activity is a part of their "lifestyle", will you feel confident in taking action to protect your employees' morale?

Remember: you don't have to be guilty to be sued. In anticipation of brisk activity, publishers are already advertising "Sexual Orientation" litigation guides to lawyers. Already, homosexuals are bringing million-dollar verdicts against employers, even when their behavior has violated the conditions of their employment.

Keep this added burden from overwhelming Colorado's business community. **Vote "YES!" on Amendment 2 this November.** ∎

AMENDMENT 2 will *not* keep gays from legal recourse, or equal protection!

In fine fear-mongering form, EPOC is claiming that after Amendment 2's passage, homosexuals will be ". . . legislatively barred from asking for or receiving protection from even basic discrimination." Sound scary? It's designed to. It's also complete nonsense.

✔ Amendment 2 will only prohibit discrimination claims *based on* sexual orientation. Homosexuals as individuals will still have legal recourse: recourse based on factors like the fact that they were good employees, minding their own business, etc. They won't — as American citizens — be "barred" from the courts.

To argue that membership in a particular group shouldn't form the basis of a discrimination claim — that's different than barring that group's members from ever making a claim on any basis. EPOC members exploit this distinction — apparently hoping it will prove beyond the understanding of the "Average Coloradan".

Example: young-Caucasian-males-without-disabilities aren't a protected class. Claims of discrimination are not accepted on the basis of being a Caucasian-male-without-disabilities. But does that mean that someone belonging to this group

has no legal recourse? Of course not. Just ask a Caucasian-male, Alan Bakke. If he hadn't had legal recourse, there wouldn't be a famous Supreme Court reverse-discrimination case named after him. For Bakke to get that recourse, however, we didn't have to make Caucasian-males a specially protected class, or declare them, as a group, immune from discrimination. That would have destroyed the whole meaning of civil-rights. And so will protected status for homosexuals.

✔ Once more for the record: anti-discrimination laws were written to protect specially protected classes — groups who've proven they need help. Caucasian-males-under-forty aren't protected by them. Millionaires-born-that-way can't file claims based on being millionaires-born-that-way. Neither should an affluent, well-educated and politically powerful group, based only on the gender of their sex partners. Anti-discrimination laws were made to protect people based on what they clearly "are", not how they behave, what kind of sexual "inclinations" they proclaim, and not, God forbid, what kind of person they sleep with. Your "YES" vote will not deprive homosexuals of a single basic right — or access to the courts. ∎

Making sense out of "discrimination"

Historically, anti-discrimination laws were written for specially protected classes — and nobody else. Caucasian males under forty aren't protected by those laws. Millionaires born that way aren't protected by those laws. These laws were made to protect disadvantaged, politically powerless people not because of how they behave or what kind of kinky desires they have. If you're not politically powerless, if there's no sign that you're actually oppressed, you don't have the privilege of claiming discrimination just because people don't like your behavior or desires.

Militant gays want to create a whole new category of anti-discrimination protections. Now they want rich, "horny", political power brokers to enjoy special protection from discrimination.

They're counting on Americans to not know what "discrimination" really means. Show the gay extremists that you know — vote YES on Amendment 2.

VOTE YES ON AMENDMENT 2

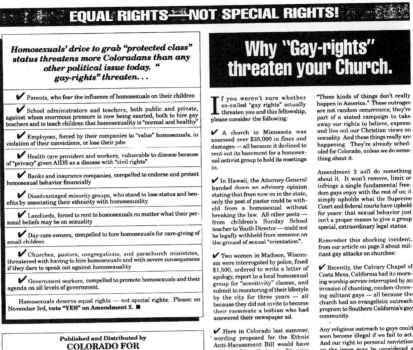

EQUAL RIGHTS—NOT SPECIAL RIGHTS!

Homosexuals' drive to grab "protected class" status threatens more Coloradans than any other political issue today. " gay-rights" threaten...

✔ Parents, who fear the influence of homosexuals on their children

✔ School administrators and teachers, both public and private, against whom enormous pressure is now being exerted, both to hire gay teachers and to teach children that homosexuality is "normal and healthy"

✔ Employees, forced by their companies to "value" homosexuals, in violation of their convictions, or lose their jobs

✔ Health care providers and workers, vulnerable to disease because of "privacy" given AIDS as a disease with "civil rights"

✔ Banks and insurance companies, compelled to endorse and protect homosexual behavior financially

✔ Disadvantaged minority groups, who stand to lose status and benefits by associating their ethnicity with homosexuality

✔ Landlords, forced to rent to homosexuals no matter what their personal beliefs may be on sexuality

✔ Day-care owners, compelled to hire homosexuals for care-giving of small children

✔ Churches, pastors, congregations, and parachurch ministries, threatened with having to hire homosexuals and with severe consequences if they dare to speak out against homosexuality

✔ Government workers, compelled to promote homosexuals and their agenda on all levels of government.

Homosexuals deserve equal rights — not special rights. Please: on November 3rd, vote "YES" on Amendment 2. ■

Published and Distributed by
COLORADO FOR FAMILY VALUES
Colorado Springs, CO

with the help of local concerned citizens

Will Perkins, Chairman, Executive Board • Kevin Tebedo, Director
© 1992 Colorado for Family Values

Why "Gay-rights" threaten your Church.

If you weren't sure whether so-called "gay rights" actually threaten you and this fellowship, please consider the following:

✔ A church in Minnesota was assessed over $35,000 in fines and damages — all because it declined to rent out its basement for a homosexual activist group to hold its meetings in.

✔ In Hawaii, the Attorney General handed down an advisory opinion stating that from now on in the state, only the post of pastor could be withheld from a homosexual without breaking the law. All other posts — from children's Sunday School teacher to Youth Director — could not be legally withheld from someone on the ground of sexual "orientation".

✔ Two women in Madison, Wisconsin were interrogated by police, fined $1,500, ordered to write a letter of apology, report to a local homosexual group for "sensitivity" classes, and submit to monitoring of their lifestyle by the city for three years — all because they did not invite to become their roommate a lesbian who had answered their newspaper ad.

✔ Here in Colorado last summer, wording proposed for the Ethnic Anti-Harassment Bill would have made it a felony "hate crime" to voice any views critical of gays. Your spiritual leader could have been subject to arrest for even reading negative towards homosexuality from the pulpit!

Please don't write these off as random events, or shake your head and think,

"These kinds of things don't really happen in America." These outrages are not random occurrences; they're part of a stated campaign to take away our rights to believe, express and live out our Christian views on sexuality. And these things really are happening. They're already scheduled for Colorado, unless we do something about it.

Amendment 2 *will* do something about it. It won't remove, limit or infringe a single fundamental freedom gays enjoy with the rest of us; it simply upholds what the Supreme Court and federal courts have upheld for years: that sexual behavior just isn't a proper reason to give a group special, extraordinary legal status.

Remember this shocking incident, from our article on page 3 about militant gay attacks on churches:

✔ Recently, the Calvary Chapel of Costa Mesa, California had its morning worship service interrupted by an invasion of chanting, condom-throwing militant gays — all because the church had an evangelical outreach program to Southern California's gay community.

Any religious outreach to gays could soon become illegal if we fail to act. And our right to personal conviction on the issue may be considered a crime.

Won't you help? Your "YES" vote for Amendment 2 will put a crucial safeguard in our constitution — a safeguard, among others things, for religious freedoms — yours and mine. ■

"WHAT HOMOSEXUALS DO AMONG THEM-SELVES IN PRIVATE, THAT'S UP TO THEM. I JUST DON'T THINK IT OUGHT TO GET 'EM SPECIAL RIGHTS , THAT'S ALL."

—That's what one crusty Coloradan told us during out petition drive. We couldn't have put it better outselves. Coloradans understand that protected class status shouldn't be given to just anyone who asks for it. That wouldn't be fair.

Amendment 2 says basically one thing: that homosexuals, like all Americans, deserve *equal rights*. But nothing about their circumstances, their lifestyle or their political power rates them as a group in need of *special* rights. Don't let "political correctness" and Hollywood values carry the day. **Vote "YES" on Amendment 2** and cast a vote for the true meaning of civil rights.

VOTE YES! ON AMENDMENT 2

7

EQUAL RIGHTS—NOT SPECIAL RIGHTS!

Don't believe "EPOC's fables". Look inside for the facts!

The largest pro-gay special rights organization calls itself "EPOC", or the "Equal Protection Only Campaign" (an intentionally deceptive title, since the organization is clearly after protected class status for homosexuals, a far cry from "equal protection only", and deceptive because Amendment 2 will leave all basic, "equal" protections homosexuals enjoy in place. If you're paying close attention to the debate over Amendment 2, you've probably run across some of EPOC's scare tactics and inaccurate claims. We call them "EPOC's fables" — but don't take our word for it. For honest-to-goodness facts about the issues surrounding Amendment 2 and the claims "EPOC" is making, consult the table below and check out the pages enclosed. It may be a real "eye-opening" experience.

EPOC's Fables	The Truth	Read about it on page:
"Amendment 2 will write discrimination into the Constitution"	Amendment 2 protects the integrity of civil-rights protections	3
"Gays are just like the rest of us"	Their lifestyle is sex-addicted and tragic	4
"Amendment 2 violates home rule"	Civil-rights isn't a home-rule issue: just ask Thurgood Marshall.	3
"Gays are oppressed"	Gays are affluent, well-educated and powerful.	1
"Amendment 2 stands for hatred of gays"	CFV has spoken out against hatred all along. Facts don't hate; they just are.	3
"Minorities should oppose Amendment 2"	Disadvantaged minorities will lose hard-won gains if gays gain protected class status.	1
"Amendment 2 will deny gays any legal recourse, ever"	Amendment 2 will deny claims based on homosexuality — gays will still have all the recourse everyone else has.	6

SECTION 3

SEXUALITY AND CITIZENSHIP IN AN INTERNATIONAL SETTING

PART B.   INTERNATIONAL OBLIGATIONS AND UNITED STATES' REGULATION OF SEXUALITY

Page 754—Add the following Postscript right after *Toonen*:

Postscript. Tasmania initially resisted repeal of its sodomy law, despite some pressure from its national government. In 1996, the lower house of Tasmania's parliament voted to repeal, but the upper house blocked the effort. In May 1997, the upper house went along with the repeal of statutes criminalizing "indecent practices between male persons" (patterned on England's 1885 law against "gross indecency" between males) and "sex against the order of nature."

PART C.   GENDER, SEXUALITY, AND ASYLUM

Page 761—Add the following decision and notes after Problem 8–6:

Alla Konstantinova Pitcherskaia v. INS, 118 F.3d 641 (9th Cir.1997). [The facts of the case are set forth in greater detail in Chapter 2, § 1 of this Supplement, pp. 32–33.] Alla Konstantinova Pitcherskaia sought asylum from Russia, ultimately on the basis of feared medical detention, and perhaps drastic electrical shock therapy, as a response to her alleged lesbian orientation and gay rights activism. The INS and then the Board of Immigration Appeals denied her application for asylum, on the ground that the Russian authorities' apparent intent was to "cure" her of what they considered a mental disease; hence, there was no "persecution" that is required for asylum.

The Ninth Circuit, in an opinion by **Judge Fletcher**, reversed. The Ninth Circuit invoked the definition of persecution developed in *Kasinga* (casebook, p. 757): "the infliction of harm or suffering by a government, or persons a government is unwilling or unable to control, to overcome a characteristic of a victim." Although the Board of Immigration Appeals has, in other cases, e.g., *In re Mogharrabi*, 19 I & N Dec. 439, 446 (BIA 1987), insisted upon a punitive intent to establish state "persecution," the Ninth Circuit held those precedents inconsistent with the statute. Dictionary definitions of the term, the remedial policy of the Refugee Act of 1980, and

101

the apparent international practice under the 1967 Protocol Relating to the Status of Refugees, 19 U.S.T. 6223, T.I.A.S. No. 6577, 606 U.N.T.S. 268 (which the 1980 statute was enacted to implement) suggest that "persecution" includes nonpunitive but harmful state actions. The Ninth Circuit rejected the views of *Faddoul v. INS*, 37 F.3d 185, 188 (5th Cir.1994), which followed *Mogharrabi*, rather than *Kasinga*, to require a showing by the alien that harm or suffering will be inflicted upon her in order to punish her for possessing a characteristic a persecutor sought to overcome.

"The fact that a persecutor believes the harm he is inflicting is 'good for' his victim does not make it any less painful to the victim, or, indeed, remove the conduct from the statutory definition of persecution. The BIA majority's requirement that an alien prove that her persecutor's subjective intent was punitive is unwarranted. Human rights laws cannot be sidestepped by simply couching actions that torture mental or physically in benevolent terms such as 'curing' or 'treating' the victims." Judge Fletcher remanded the case to the BIA to determine whether Pitcherskaia met the other statutory requirements for asylum.

NOTES ON PROBLEMS FACED BY GAY AND GENDER–BENDING ASYLUM SEEKERS

As the *Pitcherskaia* and *Tenorio* (casebook, pp. 760–61) cases reveal, lesbians, gay men, bisexuals, and even people perceived to be gay have been receiving asylum in this country throughout the decade.[f] As the Attorney General's 1994 directive on so-called "pink asylum" suggested and *Pitcherskaia* took for granted, gay people are considered "a particular social group" for purposes of the 1980 statute. Other barriers to asylum have led or will lead to denials for other gay asylum seekers, however.

1. *Persecution.* It remains to be seen whether the objective, nonpunitive standard of *Kasinga/Pitcherskaia* will prevail over the subjective, punitive standard of *Mogharrabi/Faddoul.* Even if *Pitcherskaia* prevails, it is not a simple (or inexpensive) matter for gay asylum seekers to prove persecution, and some cases are denied or never brought for lack of such proof. Moreover, if the complained-of persecution is private rather than public, the asylum seeker has a much more difficult case, for the INS generally does not approve asylum for people subjected only to local and private persecution.

2. *Problematic Activities.* The *Toboso-Alfonso* case noted in the casebook, p. 761, involved a gay man denied asylum because he had been convicted of serious nonsexual crimes. But gay men and lesbians have long

---

f. See Ryan Goodman, "The Incorporation of International Human Rights Standards into Sexual Orientation Asylum Claims: Cases of Involuntary 'Medical' Intervention," 105 *Yale L.J.* 255 (1995) (student note); Jin Park, "Pink Asylum: Political Asylum Eligibility of Gay Men and Lesbians Under U.S. Immigration Policy," 42 *UCLA L. Rev.* 1115 (1995) (student comment).

been prosecuted under nonsexual as well as sexual offenses. Alla Pitcherskaia, for example, was arrested for "hooliganism" in Russia, but she was able to show that such a charge was the standard one against sexual minorities and feminists, perhaps similar to disorderly conduct and vagrancy in American law. We do not know how the INS would react to an asylum seeker having repeated arrests in his home country for public solicitation of same-sex partners, male prostitution, or public indecency.

3.   *The New Time Limit and the Closet.* Under the Illegal Immigration Reform and Immigration Responsibility Act of 1996 and its implementing regulations, anyone seeking asylum in this country must apply to the INS within a year of their arriving in this country. This is a special problem for gay and lesbian asylum seekers, because many of them do not realize they might seek asylum because of antigay animus in their home country (Alla Pitcherskaia did not include it in her original application, for example) or, more tellingly, because many of them are afraid to "come out of the closet" in the United States.[g] Gay asylum seekers may be personally ambivalent about or even ashamed of their homosexuality, and even those personally secure in a minority sexual orientation cannot help but notice how homophobic most of the United States remains. The vast majority of the asylum seekers assisted by the New York Office of the Lesbian and Gay Immigration Rights Task Force do not come forward within a year's time. This pattern may change under the new statute, but one doubts that it will dissipate entirely.

*

g. See Kai Wright, "Experts Warn Time Running Out for Gay Refugees," *Wash. Blade*, Feb. 20, 1998, at 16.

CHAPTER 9

Families We Choose

SECTION 1

The Privatization of Family Law

PART B.   NONMARITAL OBLIGATIONS AND BENEFITS

Page 789. Add the following sentence at the end of the Postscript in paragraph 3:

For a decision allowing same-sex partners to bring suit for visitation rights to children they helped raise, see *J.A.L. v. E.P.H.*, 682 A.2d 1314 (Pa.Super.1996) (excerpted in Section 3B of this Chapter, below).

THE EXPANDING RIGHT TO MARRY

PART B.   THE SAME-SEX MARRIAGE DEBATE

Page 815. Insert the following additions at the end of Note 3 to *Baehr v. Lewin*:

The leading commentator on the choice-of-law issues raised by same-sex marriage is Barbara Cox. E.g., "Same–Sex Marriage and Choice of Law: If We Marry in Hawaii, Are We Still Married When We Return Home?," 1994 *Wis. L. Rev.* 1033. For criticism of the "public policy" exception, see Larry Kramer (not the AIDS activist Larry Kramer, by the way), "Same–Sex Marriage, Conflict of Laws, and the Unconstitutional Public Policy Exception," 106 *Yale L.J.* 1965 (1997), to which Linda Silberman, "Can the Island of Hawaii Bind the World? A Comment on Same–Sex Marriage and Federalism Values," 16 *QLR* 191 (1996), is an analytically and doctrinally strong response.

In the wake of *Baehr*, at least twenty-nine states have enacted new statutes seeking to head off recognition of "gay marriages" in their jurisdictions. As of July, 1, 1998, those states have been Alabama, Alaska, Arizona, Arkansas, Delaware, Florida, Georgia, Idaho, Illinois, Indiana, Iowa, Kansas, Kentucky, Maine, Michigan, Minnesota, Mississippi, Missouri, Montana, North Carolina, North Dakota, Oklahoma, Pennsylvania, South Carolina, South Dakota, Tennessee, Utah, Virginia, Washington. For the variety of approaches, consider these examples:[31]

● "Any marriage between persons of the same gender is prohibited and null and void from the beginning. Any marriage between persons of the same gender that is valid in another jurisdiction does not constitute a legal or valid marriage in Mississippi." 1997 Miss. Laws 301, codified at Miss. Code § 93–1–1(2).

● "Marriage between persons of the same sex is void and prohibited." 1996 Ariz. Laws ch. 348, amending Ariz. Rev. Stat. § 25–101(C).

● "The following marriages are prohibited ... (5) a marriage between 2 individuals of the same sex." and "Same-sex marriages: public policy. A marriage between 2 individuals of the same sex is contrary to the public

---

31. Most of the state statutes are reprinted as an appendix to Andrew Koppelman, "Same–Sex Marriage and Public Policy: The Miscegenation Precedents," 16 *QLR* 105, 134–51 (1996).

policy of this State." 1996 Ill. Laws 89–459, codified at Ill. Comp. Stat. §§ 5/212(a)(5) and 5/213.1.

Would these statutes successfully bar recognition of Hawaiian same-sex marriages in Mississippi, Arizona, and Illinois, respectively? Are they all equally consistent (or inconsistent) with the Full Faith and Credit Clause?

Most of the statutes also make clear that same-sex marriages are not authorized under the marriage laws of their jurisdictions.[a] Some of the statutes enacted after mid–1996 also provide that the terms "marriage" and "spouse," when used in the state code or by state agencies, can only mean different-sex couples. E.g., 1997 Fla. Laws ch. 97–268, codified at Fla. Stat. § 741.212.

Page 816. In Problem 9–3, strike sentence two of the first paragraph and insert the following in its place:

DOMA is Public Law 104–199, 110 Stat. 2419. Section 3 of DOMA creates new 1 U.S.C. § 7: "In determining the meaning of any Act of Congress, or of any ruling, regulation, or interpretation of the various administrative bureaus and agencies of the United States, the word 'marriage' means only a legal union between one man and one woman as husband and wife, and the word 'spouse' refers only to a person of the opposite sex who is a husband or a wife." [Continue with "Section 2" * * *]

Page 817. Insert the following new paragraphs at the end of Problem 9–3, and then add the *Baehr* case (on remand) and some postscripts:

In addition to the already noted argument that Congress did not have authority under the Full Faith and Credit Clause to override state recognition requirements of that clause in DOMA § 2, critical commentators have objected that DOMA (1) invades or usurps family law rules left to the states as inherently local matters by the Tenth Amendment, (2) creates statutory "sex discriminations" that violate the Equal Protection Clause (as in *Baehr*), and/or (3) is merely a reflection of antigay animus of the sort rejected as a basis for state action in *Romer v. Evans* (casebook, pp. 93–105).[b] Why did the Clinton Administration not address these arguments in

---

a. This move, by the way, is nothing new. Ever since the first same-sex marriage "scare," in the 1970s, states have been enacting laws to make clear that marriage was limited to "one man and one woman," to assure that lesbian and gay couples could not marry in their jurisdictions. E.g., 1977 Cal. Stat. ch. 339, §§ 1–2 (codified at Cal. Civ. Code §§ 4100, 4101[a]); 1991 Conn. Acts 91–50, § 36 (state gay rights law) (codified at Conn. Gen. Stat. § 46A–81R); 1987 La. Acts 886 (codified at La. Civ. Code art. 89); 1984 Md. Laws 296 (codified at Md. Code, Family Law § 2–201); 1993 Minn. Laws ch. 22, § 7

(state gay rights law) (codified at Minn. Stat. § 363.021); 1975 Va. Acts ch. 644 (codified at Va. Code § 20–45.2). Some of these same states have, in 1996 and 1997, enacted fresh new laws to respond to the Hawaii litigation.

b. See Andrew Koppelman, "Dumb and DOMA: Why the Defense of Marriage Act Is Unconstitutional," 83 *Iowa L. Rev.* (1997); Evan Wolfson & Michael Melcher, "Constitutional and Legal Defects in the 'Defense of Marriage' Act," 16 *QLR* 221 (1996), as well as Scott Ruskay–Kidd, "The Defense of Marriage Act and the Overextension of Congres-

its Justice Department letter? Are they persuasive as to either section of DOMA?

In evaluating these arguments, consider the congressional debate: What were Congress and the President trying to accomplish? After brief hearings, DOMA was adopted by lopsided majorities in both chambers of Congress and signed by the President (in a midnight ceremony). Opponents of DOMA argued that, until same-sex marriages were actually recognized in some state, DOMA was premature and unnecessary legislation whose only purpose was to scapegoat gay people. See 142 Cong. Rec. S10112 (Sen. Boxer) (daily ed. Sept. 10, 1996); id. at H7273 (Rep. Schroeder), H7278 (Rep. Frank) (daily ed. July 11, 1996). Some DOMA supporters spoke of same-sex marriage in apocalyptic terms as foreboding the end of western civilization, e.g., id. at H7482 (Rep. Barr), H7486 (Rep. Buyer) (daily ed. July 12, 1996). Many of the DOMA supporters favored the legislation as a way to save marriage as an institution. "Gay marriage" would hasten the decline of marriage, in part because polygamous or incestuous unions would then also have to be recognized.

Most of the key supporters emphasized what are called "no promo homo" arguments, such as this: "Should the law express its neutrality between homosexual and heterosexual relationships? . . . Should Congress tell the children of America that it is a matter of indifference whether they establish families with a partner of the opposite sex or cohabit with someone of the same sex?" *Id.* at H7491 (Rep. Canady) (July 12, 1996). The most eloquent articulation of this idea in the House was by Representative Henry Hyde, *id.* at H7500–H7501 (daily ed. Sept. 12, 1996). DOMA supporters insisted that their position was not one of intolerance. "Tolerance does not require us to say that all lifestyles are morally equal." *Id.* at S10114 (daily ed. Sept. 10, 1996) (Sen. Coats).

Would the foregoing arguments pass muster under the rational-basis-with-bite scrutiny of *Romer*? Under the heightened scrutiny of the VMI Case (if DOMA were held to create a sex discrimination in the law)? How should the Tenth Amendment argument cut?

Soon after DOMA was enacted (in September 1996), Hawaii did move one step closer to issuing marriage licenses.

Ninia Baehr, Genora Dancel, et al. v. Lawrence H. Miike, 1996 WL 694235 (Hawaii Cir. Ct., 1st Cir.1996). In the midst of the controversy occasioned by DOMA and reactions in other states as well as Hawaii, *Baehr* went back to the trial court. In the autumn of 1996, **Judge Chang** held a bench trial on the state's effort to overcome the presumption that its refusal to grant marriage licenses to same-sex couples is unconstitutional. In accord with the state supreme court mandate, as clarified on May 27, 1993, the state asserted that the sex-based classification "furthers compelling state interests and is narrowly drawn to avoid unnecessary abridg-

sional Authority," 97 *Colum. L. Rev.* 1435 (1997) (student note).

ments of constitutional rights." In its legal papers, the state relied on a variety of public interests to justify the sex discrimination, including "fostering procreation within a marital setting" and "protecting the State's public fisc from the reasonably foreseeable effects of State approval of same-sex marriage," but its main argument and all its witnesses spoke to "protecting the health and welfare of children and other persons." Trial Court Finding of Fact ("FF") No. 18, *Baehr v. Miike.*

The state presented four expert witnesses, the most prominent of whom was Dr. Kyle Pruett, a Yale University expert in child development. He testified that children who are raised by same-sex parents have an overabundance of information about one gender and too little information about the other gender (FF No. 27) but admitted on cross-examination that "same-sex parents can, and do, produce children with a clear sense of gender identity" (FF No. 28). "It is Dr. Pruett's opinion that most children are more likely to reach their optimal development being raised in an intact family by their mother and father." (FF No. 30.) "However Dr. Pruett also stated that single parents, gay fathers, lesbian mothers, and same-sex couples have the potential to, and often do, raise children that are happy, healthy, and well-adjusted." (FF No. 31.) "Dr. Pruett agreed that, in general, gay and lesbian parents are as fit and loving parents as non-gay persons and couples." (FF No. 34.)

Although not making as many concessions to the capabilities of lesbian and gay parents, the state's other expert witnesses testified along the same lines as Dr. Pruett. Dr. David Eggebeen, a sociologist, testified that children raised in a single-parent and step-parent homes are at a "heightened risk" of economic hardship, behavioral and academic problems, and teenage pregnancies (FF Nos. 46–47). As evidence of dysfunctional step-parent families, Dr. Eggebeen recalled the story of Cinderella (FF No. 48). Like Dr. Pruett, Dr. Eggebeen testified that lesbian and gay couples can and often do make excellent parents (FF No. 52) and should be allowed to adopt children (FF No. 53). Finally, he testified that cohabiting same-sex couples are less stable than married couples (FF No. 54) and concluded that "children of same-sex couples would be helped if their families had access to or were able to receive the following benefits of marriage: (1) state income tax advantages; (2) public assistance; (3) enforcement of child support; (4) inheritance rights; and (5) the ability to prosecute wrongful death actions. Dr. Eggebeen also agreed that children of same-sex couples would be helped if their families received the social status derived from marriage." (FF No. 55.)

Plaintiffs also presented four expert witnesses, the chief of whom were Dr. Pepper Schwartz, a sociologist who has coauthored a major study of families and relationships, *American Couples*, and Dr. Charlotte Patterson, whose studies and expert opinions are expressed in her law review article digested in the casebook, pp. 846–47. Dr. Schwartz testified that lesbian and gay couples want to marry for reasons of interpersonal commitment and family formation (FF No. 80). She testified that same-sex marriage would have a positive impact on society and the institution of marriage (FF No. 87). Dr. Patterson testified that her comparative studies demonstrated that children raised in same-sex households developed the same as those raised in different-sex households, except that the former children were more likely to express symptoms of stress in their lives (FF No. 91). Dr. Pruett, the state's witness, expressed "his agreement with the general conclusions reached by Dr. Patterson. More specifically, Dr. Pruett agreed with the following conclusions, that gay and lesbian parents 'are doing a good job' and that the 'kids are turning out just fine.' Dr. Pruett was not surprised by Dr. Patterson's conclusions. In fact, they are what he expected to see, and although Dr. Pruett questions Dr. Patterson's research methodology, he is not aware of any data, research or literature which disputes Dr. Patterson's findings and conclusions." (FF No. 38.)

Based upon the foregoing evidence, Judge Chang entered specific findings of fact and law as pertaining to his mandate on remand. Because the state essentially presented no evidence, Judge Chang summarily rejected all of the state's interests except the protection of children claim (FF Nos. 117–119). As to this last interest, Judge Chang found that "an intact family environment consisting of a child and his or her mother and father presents a less burdened environment for the development of a happy, healthy and well-adjusted child" (FF No. 122).

"123. However, there is diversity in the structure and configuration of families. In Hawaii, and elsewhere, children are being raised by their natural parents, single parents, step-parents, grandparents, adopted parents, hanai parents, foster parents, gay and lesbian parents, and same-sex couples. * * *

"125. The evidence presented by Plaintiffs and Defendant establishes that the single most important factor in the development of a happy, healthy and well-adjusted child is the nurturing relationship between parent and child. * * *

"126. The sexual orientation of parents does not automatically disqualify them from being good, fit, loving or successful parents.

"127. The sexual orientation of parents is not in and of itself a indicator of the overall adjustment and development of children. * * *

"132. Gay and lesbian parents and same-sex couples can be as fit and loving parents, as non-gay men and women and different-sex couples. * * *

"135. As noted herein, there is a benefit to children which comes from being raised by their mother and father in an intact and relatively stress-free home.

"However, in this case, Defendant has not proved that allowing same-sex marriage will probably result in significant differences in development or outcomes of children raised by gay or lesbian parents and same-sex couples, as compared to children raised by different-sex couples or their biological parents. * * *

"136. Contrary to Defendant's assertions, if same-sex marriage is allowed, the children being raised by gay or lesbian parents and same-sex couples may be assisted, because they may obtain certain protections and benefits that come with or become available as a result of marriage. See *Baehr v. Lewin*, 74 Haw. 530, 560–561, 852 P.2d 44, 59 (1993), for a list of noteworthy marital rights and benefits. * * *

"139. Simply put, Defendant has failed to establish or prove that the public interest in the well-being of children and families, or the optimal development of children will be adversely affected by same-sex marriage."

Based upon the foregoing Findings of Fact and the Conclusions of Law mandated by the Hawaii Supreme Court decision in *Baehr v. Lewin*, Judge Chang entered judgment for plaintiffs and an injunction against the state's enforcement of its discrimination against same-sex couples.

Postscripts: (1) Judge Chang's injunction has been stayed pending the state's appeal of his judgment. As of July 1, 1998, the Hawaii Supreme Court has not ruled on the state's appeal. Is there any basis for reversing Judge Chang?

(2) In a complicated set of compromises, the Hawaii legislature in April 1997 enacted two measures: one creating legal benefits (survivorship and other property rights, some health benefits, the right to sue in some cases of tort and wrongful death of one's partner) to couples who register as *reciprocal beneficiaries*, and a second placing a proposed constitutional amendment on the ballot for November 3, 1998. If adopted, new Article I, § 23 of the Hawaii Constitution would read: "The legislature shall have the power to reserve marriage to opposite-sex couples." If the amendment passes and the supreme court affirms Judge Chang, then the legislature could, apparently, override the supreme court's decision and reinstate the ban, if it chooses to exercise the power given it. Is this subject to any kind of federal constitutional attack?

(3) In parallel developments, the Alaska legislature in May 1998 voted to pose to that state's voters a ballot initiative that would amend the state constitution to limit legal recognition to marriages that involve "one man and one woman." The initiative was a response to a February 1998 ruling by state Superior Court Judge Peter Michalski that Alaska cannot deny marriage licenses to same-sex couples unless it can demonstrate a "compelling" reason for the denial. *Brause v. Bureau of Vital Statistics*, 1998 WL 88743 (Alaska Super.). In May, 1998, the state supreme court declined to hear an interlocutory appeal and remanded for a trial. A similar lawsuit seeking same-sex marriage is pending in the Vermont Supreme Court. See *Stan Baker and Peter Harrigan et al. v. State of Vermont*, No. 98–32.

PART C.   THE CONSTITUTIONALITY OF OTHER RESTRICTIONS

Page 825.   Insert the following sentences at the end of Note 1 on Polygamy:

For a response to Strassberg and an argument that polygamy, like same-sex marriage, has been unfairly vilified, see David Chambers, "Polygamy and Same–Sex Marriage," 26 *Hofstra L. Rev.* 53 (1997). For a detailed, and also sympathetic, historical treatment of Mormon polygamists and the federal *Kulturkampf* against them in the 1880s and 1890s, see William Eskridge, Jr., "A Jurisprudence of 'Coming Out': Religion, Homosexuality, and Collisions of Liberty and Equality in American Public Law," 106 *Yale L.J.* 2411 (1997).

SECTION 3

CHILDREN IN FAMILIES OF CHOICE

PART A. STATE DECISIONS ABOUT PLACEMENT OF CHILDREN

Page 837. Insert the following at the end of Note 2 to *Conkel*:

A number of recent state appellate decisions have allowed trial court restrictions on visitation by lesbian mothers or gay fathers involved in ongoing same-sex relationships. See, e.g., *Ex parte D.W.W.*, ___ So.2d ___, 1998 WL 81615 (Ala.1998) (upholding trial court restrictions on visitation by mother, "in order to limit the children's exposure to their mother's lesbian lifestyle"); *Hertzler v. Hertzler*, 908 P.2d 946 (Wyo.1995) (upholding restrictions on gay mother's visitation so that strife between her and the father and his new wife could be minimized). On the other hand, such restriction-on-visitation cases have diminished in some jurisdictions because of appellate disapproval of them. Even in southern jurisdictions, such restrictions are sometimes rejected. See *In re R.E.W.*, 471 S.E.2d 6 (Ga. App.), review denied, 472 S.E.2d 295 (Ga.1996).

Page 841. Insert the following Note right after the *Bottoms* decision:

NOTE ON REVA SIEGAL'S THEORY OF MODERNIZED JUSTIFICATION AND NEW REASONS FOR DENYING LESBIAN AND GAY CUSTODY

Reva Siegal, "'The Rule of Love': Wife Beating as Prerogative and Privacy," 105 *Yale L.J.* 2117 (1996), argues from women's experience with spousal battering that even when law is "reformed" in response to complaints by formerly marginalized groups, the oppressive practices continue and are reaffirmed through a "modernization of justification." By defending practices in terms that are more persuasive to a new generation, modernized justifications can actually strengthen oppressive practices.[c] The caselaw analyzing gay and lesbian custody claims might be analyzed under Siegal's theory.[d]

---

c. Husbands' battering of wives came under attack in the nineteenth century, and wives gained the "right" to sue their husbands for assault. In the latter half of the century, courts still denied relief, upon theories of privacy which insulated the family from legal intervention.

d. See William Eskridge, Jr., *Gaylaw: Challenging the Apartheid of the Closet* ch. 8 (forthcoming Harv. U. Press, 1999).

Note the analytic progression by the different courts evaluating Sharon Bottoms' claim to custody of her son: (1) the trial judge relied on Bottoms' sexual orientation and the "illegality" of her homosexual conduct under Virginia's sodomy law as the basis for depriving Bottoms of custody (casebook, p. 839); (2) the intermediate appellate court took a libertarian position, requiring tangible evidence of harm to the child and finding none sufficient to support a shift in custody (casebook, p. 840); and (3) the state supreme court considered Bottoms' lesbianism only one consideration and refocused the case on allegations of neglect and unhealthy practices on the part of the mother and her partner (casebook, pp. 840–41). This progression reflects the familiar oscillation between *status* and *conduct*: progay positions focus on the former and insist that it is irrelevant (*Romer v. Evans*; the intermediate court in *Bottoms*), while antigay positions focus on the latter and penalize gay people for engaging in it (*Bowers v. Hardwick*; the supreme court in *Bottoms*).

Within the category of conduct, there has been a Siegal-like shift in justifying reason, from an old-fashioned focus on *unnatural acts* which render a parent *per se* unfit to have custody (the Virginia trial court), to a modernized focus on *harmful acts* which create problems for children who are in the most vulnerable position. See also Lynn Wardle, "The Potential Impact of Homosexual Parenting on Children," 1997 *U. Ill. L. Rev.* 833 (digested below). A similar shift can be observed in other state appellate decisions which deny custody to lesbian or gay parents, but which strikingly distance their reasoning from harsh trial court rhetoric. See *Tucker v. Tucker*, 910 P.2d 1209 (Utah 1996), and *Scott v. Scott*, 665 So.2d 760 (La.App.1995), where appellate courts deemphasized the parent's homosexuality and emphasized the gay parent's extramarital cohabitation with a same-sex partner; *Ward v. Ward*, 1996 WL 491692 (Fla.App.1996) (unpublished), where the courts transferred custody to a father convicted of murdering his first wife, from a lesbian mother whose sexual conduct the appellate court found was hurting the child.

Within the subcategory of harmful acts, there is some emphasis on the idea of a *harmful lifestyle*. The cases where courts impose limitations on visitation by lesbian and gay parents are most dramatic. Trial judges continue to condition visitation on the lesbian or gay parent's willingness to forego open displays of affection or cohabitation with same-sex partners. Illustrative, but perhaps extreme, is *Ex parte D.W.W.*, ___ So.2d ___, 1998 WL 81615 (Ala.1998). The trial court had directed visitation by the lesbian mother to occur only in the home of the child's grandparents and under their control and supervision. The state intermediate appellate court reversed, but the state supreme court reinstated the trial court's restrictions "in order to limit the children's exposure to their mother's lesbian lifestyle." Although the trial court had based its order on its factual finding that the children had already been harmed by exposure to same-sex affection between the mother and her same-sex partner, the supreme court ruled that exposure to the lesbian lifestyle was inherently detrimental to children.

Page 848. Insert the following article digests right after the Patterson article (both articles are worth reading in their entirety for a full explication of the debate):

Lynn Wardle, "The Potential Impact of Homosexual Parenting on Children," 1997 *U. Ill. L. Rev.* **833**. Family law Professor Lynn Wardle's article is the first major effort by a legal scholar to challenge the view expressed in Dr. Patterson's article (casebook, pp. 846–47). The thesis of his article is that courts should apply the "best interests of the child" test with a policy-based presumption *against* custody by lesbian or gay parents. His analysis is both normative and empirical.

Wardle first seeks to reorient the debate about legal recognition of same-sex relationships, including marriages. He objects that the legal literature is too "adult-rights" focused and needs to return to a focus on the welfare of children. He is particularly critical of constitutional arguments, such as those based on *Romer v. Evans* (casebook, pp. 93–105). Equal rights for gay and lesbian *parents* threatens to overshadow the actual welfare of *children*. Wardle draws on the recent "registered partnership" laws of Denmark and other Scandinavian countries (casebook, p. 794), which separate issues of adult relationships, sanctioned by those laws, and adoption by same-sex couples, which are not sanctioned by those laws.

Most of the article consists of criticisms of the social science literature, surveyed by Dr. Patterson (casebook, pp. 846–47), that has found no fundamental differences between children raised in same-sex households and those raised in different-sex ones. Wardle makes several methodological criticisms: (1) the comparative (same-sex versus different-sex households) studies have relied on small and nonrandom samples, limitations that have been explicitly recognized in the studies themselves;[e] (2) the researchers start off biased in favor of "homosexual parenting" and so end up with results that support their preexisting biases; and (3) some experts have found tangible harms to children who have been raised in same-sex households.

Wardle argues from social science and other evidence that children will be harmed by same-sex parents because (1) such parents engage in immoral extramarital conduct, which will induce their children to be promiscuous and indeed develop "homosexual interests and behaviors"; (2) even when

---

e. Most of the studies state at the outset that they offer only provisional conclusions given their small and necessarily nonrandom samples. E.g., Susan Golombok and Fiona Tasker, "Do Parents Influence the Sexual Orientation of Their Children?," 32 *Dev. Psychol.* 3, 8 (1996) (impossibility of recruiting a random sample of gay parents because of the closetry of most); Charlotte Patterson, "Children of Lesbian and Gay Parents," 63 *Child Dev.* 1025, 1036–1039 (1992) (survey of the studies, including those of the author).

they do not become identifiable "homosexuals," the children of such households tend to depart from and to be confused about traditional gender roles; and (3) some children will be sexually molested by their gay parents. Given all these risks, Wardle urges extreme caution before placing a child in a "homosexual" environment and recommends a rebuttable, or possibly irrebuttable, presumption against custody or adoption by lesbian or gay parents.

Carlos Ball and Janice Pea, "Warring with Wardle: Morality, Social Science, and Gay and Lesbian Parents," 1998 *U. Ill. L. Rev.* ___. This article is a response to Professor Wardle's article. Professor Ball and Ms. Pea also start with a normative argument: Wardle's article follows traditional anti-homosexual discourse by choosing to view lesbian and gay parents mainly through the "prism of sexuality." By contrasting children as "innocent victims" of "selfish homosexuals," Wardle builds his argument from the beginning on stereotypes. According to Ball and Pea, lesbian and gay parents want children for the same reasons straight parents do— the desire to nurture, the freshness of new life, the ability to help perpetuate the human species, and so forth. Judges from a variety of perspectives in the second-parent adoption cases (casebook, pp. 861–68) have found, as a factual matter, that same-sex couples rely on the same other-regarding reasons for child-rearing that different-sex couples do.[f]

Ball and Pea agree with Wardle (and Dr. Patterson) that individual social science studies are limited by small sample size and hard-to-compare family environments. Some of the limitations have been ameliorated by studies not mentioned by Wardle; for example, a meta-analysis correcting for small sample size (but not for nonrandomness) found that the data "indicate no difference between homosexual and heterosexual parents."[g] In an ironic twist, Wardle's criticisms of social science technique apply most strongly to his own evidence against lesbian and gay parenting. Thus, argue Ball and Pea, only a few small-sample studies suggest that gay parents raise gay children, and the larger-sample studies find the incidence of homosexuality in such children to be 0% to 9%, arguably within the normal distribution in society. Wardle's charge that "homosexual parenting" will expose children to sexual molestation is refuted by statistics showing child molestation overwhelmingly perpetrated by straight men, with lesbians as well as straight women least likely to engage in such activities. Ball and Pea find no support among professional groups or elsewhere for Wardle's serious charge that the researchers are biased. Some

---

f. For a more detailed argument about the morality of same-sex relationships and families, see Carlos Ball, "Moral Foundations for a Discourse on Same–Sex Marriage: Looking Beyond Political Liberalism," 85 *Geo. L.J.* 1872 (1997).

g. Mike Allen & Nancy Burrell, "Comparing the Impact of Homosexual and Heter-osexual Parents on Children: Meta–Analysis of Existing Research," 32 *J. Homosexuality* 19, 28–30 (1996), correcting for some problems identified by Philip Belcastro et al., "A Review of Data Based Studies Addressing the Affects of Homosexual Parenting on Children's Sexual and Social Functioning," 20 *J. Divorce & Remarriage* 105 (1993).

of the researchers, such as Dr. Patterson of the University of Virginia, have received tenure based on this work at universities regarded as socially conservative.

Ball and Pea maintain that "the social science literature, despite its shortcomings, supports the rather limited proposition that gay and lesbian parents (or prospective parents) are entitled to be evaluated individually on the basis of their ability to be good parents instead of being assessed based on assumptions about their sexual orientation." See also Mark Strasser, *Legally Wed: Same–Sex Marriage and the Constitution* (1997), and "Legislative Presumptions and Judicial Assumptions: On Parenting, Adoption, and the Best Interest of the Child," 45 *Kan. L. Rev.* 49 (1996).

PART B.   SURROGACY AND ARTIFICIAL INSEMINATION

Page 861. Insert the following case and notes right before Part C:

J.A.L. v. E.P.H., 682 A.2d 1314 (Pa.Super.1996). JAL and EPH, both women, entered into a sexual relationship in 1980 and began living as life partners in 1982. In June 1991, EPH bore a child conceived by artificial insemination, assisted at every stage by JAL. When registering the child's birth, EPH gave JAL's surname as the child's middle name. The couple also signed documents recognizing JAL as the joint "guardian" of the child and gave her power to consent to medical procedures for the child. "It is our intention that [JAL] will establish a loving and parental relationship with the child," said the first document, and JAL did in fact participate in the child's early rearing. In late 1991, the women's relationship soured, and EPH moved out of their joint home. Although JAL continued to see the child in twice-weekly visitations, EPH terminated those in 1994. JAL sued for joint custody.

Following the New York Court of Appeals' decision in *Alison D.* (casebook, p. 789), the trial court held that a mother's former same-sex partner has no standing (i.e., no legal right) to seek continued connection with a child she helped raise. In an opinion by **Judge Beck**, the Pennsylvania appellate court reversed. Judge Beck agreed with the trial judge that rules against third-party standing in child custody cases serve not only to protect the court system against overloading, but also "to prevent intrusion into the protected domain of the family by those who are merely strangers, however well-meaning."

"Biological parents have a prima facie right to custody, but biological parenthood is not the only source of such a right. Cognizable rights to seek full or partial custody may also arise under statutes such as Chapter 53 of the Domestic Relations Code (permitting grandparents and greatgrandparents to seek visitation or partial custody of their grandchildren or great-grandchildren), or by virtue of the parties' conduct, as in cases where a third party who has stood in loco parentis has been recognized as possessing a prima facie right sufficient to grant standing to litigate questions of custody of the child for whom he or she has cared. * * *

" * * * [W]hile it is presumed that a child's best interest is served by maintaining the family's privacy and autonomy, that presumption must give way where the child has established strong psychological bonds with a person who, although not a biological parent, has lived with the child and provided care, nurture, and affection, assuming in the child's eye a stature like that of a parent. Where such a relationship is shown, our courts recognize that the child's best interest requires that the third party be granted standing so as to have the opportunity to litigate fully the issue of whether that relationship should be maintained even over a natural parent's objections. * * *

"In today's society, where increased mobility, changes in social mores and increased individual freedom have created a wide spectrum of arrangements filling the role of the traditional nuclear family, flexibility in the application of standing principles is required in order to adapt those principles to the interests of each particular child.[3]" [Based upon the deep and multifarious connections between JAL and the child, and the intent of both women that they share responsibility for the child's rearing, the lower court erred in denying standing. Judge Beck remanded for a hearing on whether JAL should be granted partial custody.]

NOTE ON EQUITABLE PARENTHOOD AND CUSTODY DISPUTES BETWEEN FORMER PARTNERS

The *in loco parentis* idea invoked by Judge Beck is similar to the concept of an "equitable parent": a court will treat as a parent someone who has bonded with the child and acted "as though" she were a parent. Many of the early cases have involved grandparents, and states like Pennsylvania have codified their rights statutorily. Like Chief Judge Kaye, dissenting in *Alison D.* (casebook, p. 789), Judge Beck recognized the equitable rights of someone who has, functionally, helped create a family of choice.

Counterarguments are these: (1) There may be a slippery slope: Can anybody be an equitable parent? Courts such as the one in *Holtzman* (casebook, p. 789) have defined the equitable parent functionally, in light of the extent and nature of the person's connection with the child (compare *Braschi*, casebook, pp. 787–88), but there is still a question as to who might

---

3. See generally, Katharine T. Bartlett, "Rethinking Parenthood as an Exclusive Status: The Need for Legal Alternatives When the Premise of the Nuclear Family Has Failed, 70 *Va.L.Rev.* 879 (1984); Nancy D. Polikoff, "This Child Does Have Two Mothers: Redefining Parenthood to Meet the Needs of Children in Lesbian–Mother and Other Nontraditional Families, 78 *Geo.L.J.* 459 (1990); Elizabeth A. Delaney, "Statutory Protection of the Other Mother: Legally Recognizing the Relationship Between the Nonbiological Lesbian Parent and Her Child," 43 *Hastings L.J.* 177 (1991). * * *

qualify: A babysitter? An aunt, uncle, cousin? If the list becomes too long, there is potential for terrible disruption in the mother-child family (there are few things more destructive than being involved in a domestic relations lawsuit!). (2) Relatedly, if the legislature has demarcated grandparents as people who can seek custody or visitation, like parents, why shouldn't the court limit the concept to the statutorily defined persons? The legislature is authorized to draw these kind of lines, and it is democratically accountable as well. (Is that an advantage?) (3) In states with sodomy laws (Virginia rather than Pennsylvania, for example), there might be an argument that JAL's claim would be contrary to public policy: do not "reward" lesbians with possible custody. Or allowing a *de facto* parenthood lawsuit constitutes a state "sanction" for a relationship the state has, or should, condemned.

The first two arguments against equitable parenthood for a same-sex partner were the basis for the decision in *Titchenal v. Dexter*, 693 A.2d 682 (Vt.1997), excerpted below.

PART C.   SECOND-PARENT ADOPTIONS

Page 868. Insert the following materials at the end of Problem 9–6:

Like the D.C. Court of Appeals in *M.M.D.* (casebook, pp. 863–66), the New York Court of Appeals in *Jacob* permitted the second-parent adoption. The opinion for the court was written by Chief Judge Kaye, who had dissented in *Alison D.* (casebook, p. 789). The trend is toward recognition of second-parent adoptions. In addition to the cases noted in casebook, pp. 866–67, courts in states like California have been granting them in unreported decisions.

An interesting twist occurred in Vermont. Its supreme court recognized a second-parent adoption in *In re B.L.V.B.*, 628 A.2d 1271 (Vt.1993). An amendment to override *B.L.V.B.* was rejected in the Vermont legislature, which instead codified the result in a statutory recodification enacted in 1995. 15A V.S.A. § 1–102(b). Note how this statutory change affected the doctrine of equitable parenthood in a recent Vermont case.

Chris Titchenal v. Diane Dexter, 693 A.2d 682 (Vt.1997). Diane Dexter in 1991 adopted Sarah, whom she named Sarah Dexter–Titchenal in deference to her partnership with Chris Titchenal. Titchenal cared for Sarah about 65% of the time and was called mommy by the child (as was Dexter). After the women's relationship ended in late 1994, Dexter cut off contact between Sarah and Titchenal, who sued for visitation rights in superior court. In an opinion by **Chief Justice Allen**, the Vermont Supreme Court ruled that there was no basis for an equitable parenthood claim in this appealing case.

The Chief Justice started with the proposition that "there is no common-law history of Vermont courts interfering with the rights and responsibilities of fit parents absent statutory authority to do so." Unlike

Judge Beck in *J.A.L.*, Chief Justice Allen found that the statutory regulation of nonparents' rights strongly militated against exercising a new common law power. In 1984, the Vermont legislature created statutory rights for putative fathers to sue to establish paternity (and possible custody/visitation), 15 V.S.A. §§ 301–306, and for grandparents and great-grandparents to seek visitation of their grandchildren and great-grandchildren. 15 V.S.A. §§ 1011–1016. In 1996 (effective date), the legislature codified the result in *B.L.V.B.* "Thus, same-sex couples may participate in child-rearing and have recourse to the courts in the event a custody or visitation dispute results from the breakup of a relationship."

But the existence of legislatively determined instances where nonparents could sue for visitation and where same-sex partners could establish rights as adoptive parents (which would, in turn, entitle them to seek custody or visitation in the event of a breakup of the adult relationship), militated against the court's creating an additional claim for relief. "Given the complex social and practical ramifications of expanding the classes of persons entitled to assert parental rights by seeking custody or visitation, the Legislature is better equipped to deal with the problem."

Justice Morse dissented. He accepted the majority's proposition that "equitable parentage" was inconsistent with the statutory scheme but argued, in this case, for application of "equitable adoption," under *Whitchurch v. Perry*, 408 A.2d 627 (Vt.1979). That doctrine allows foster children who were never formally adopted to participate in an estate if it can be shown that the decedent had an intent or desire to adopt the child. "The purpose of the doctrine * * * is to allow a court to find, in retrospect, an intent to adopt by a particular person who had never formally done so, for the purpose of achieving a just result." Because Titchenal had expressed a desire to adopt Sarah in 1991 (before *B.L.V.B.*) but had not done so because she thought adoption would not be approved, Justice Morse would have remanded the case to family court, to determine whether she could proceed on a theory of equitable adoption.

CHAPTER 10

SEXUALITY AND GENDER IN THE WORKPLACE

SECTION 1

GOVERNMENT EMPLOYMENT

PART B.   SEXUAL ORIENTATION DISCRIMINATION

6.   Page 895—Add the following to Note 2:

In May, 1998, President Clinton amended Executive Order No. 11,478, the order providing anti-discrimination protections for federal employees, by adding sexual orientation to the list of prohibited bases for discrimination. Executive Order No. 13,087 (May 29, 1998).

SECTION 2

THE STATUTORY BAN AGAINST SEX DISCRIMINATION

PART A. PREGNANCY DISCRIMINATION UNDER TITLE VII

Page 912–913–Add the following to Note 2:

Two appellate courts have reached opposite results in challenges to the exclusion of gay Scouts and Scoutmasters by the Boy Scouts. An intermediate appellate court in New Jersey struck down the policy, holding that the plaintiff's honesty in coming out did not render him a bad role model. *Dale v. Boy Scouts of America*, 308 N.J.Super. 516, 706 A.2d 270 (N.J.Super.1998). The California Supreme Court ruled that the Boy Scouts was not a public accommodation and thus not obligated to comply with California's civil rights law; it did not reach the role model defense. *Curran v. Mt. Diablo Council of the Boy Scouts of America,* 72 Cal.Rptr.2d 410, 952 P.2d 218 (Cal.1998). See Chapter 5 of this Supplement, pp. 58–65, for excerpts from the two decisions.

PART C SEXUAL HARASSMENT LAW

Page 921. Insert the following as the second full paragraph on this page:

As to employer liability for all kinds of sexual harassment (*quid pro quo* and hostile work environment), the Supreme Court has set forth legislative-style rules in *Faragher v. City of Boca Raton*, 118 S.Ct. 2275 (1998), and *Burlington Indus. v. Ellerth*, 118 S.Ct. 2257 (1998). When there has been a tangible job detriment (e.g., discharge, demotion), an employer is vicariously liable for sexual harassment of an employee by her or his supervisor or by a successively higher authority over the employee. When there has not been a tangible job detriment, an employer is vicariously liable, subject to affirmative defenses, viz., that the employer exercised reasonable care to prevent and correct promptly any sexually harassing behavior and that plaintiff unreasonably failed to take advantage of any preventive or corrective opportunities provided by the employer. The Court's rulemaking is considered likely to open up opportunities for victims of sexual harassment to bring suit, for many circuit court decisions were more restrictive.

Page 926–Insert the following immediately after the *Burns* decision:

NOTES ON "TRADITIONAL" SEXUAL HARASSMENT

1. *Who's the norm?* In *Burns*, the appeals court finds that a reasonable person would have found the alleged conduct to have been sufficiently severe to contaminate the workplace, but remands for the district court to determine whether Burns was herself a reasonable person for purposes of that inquiry. Should such an assessment be subjective or objective? What if the evidence proved that she had been raised in a very sheltered environment and thus became extremely upset even by non-severe actions?

2. *Meanings of "Sex."* The district court in *Burns* found that "the harassment, because it was sexual, was based on [plaintiff's] sex." Does the word "sex" in that sentence mean sexual conduct, sexual desire or sexual category? In general, in heterosexual cases, courts have reasoned that because the defendant wanted to have sex (conduct), and is implicitly presumed to be heterosexual (desire), he (in the typical case) targets the victim based on her (anatomic) sex (category). Generally, the same analysis works when the hostile conduct or speech is sexualized but not expressive of desire to have sex. For example, calling someone a sexual epithet would usually be related to his or her anatomic sex because most such epithets apply only to women or only to men. What if the conduct was sexualized but not necessarily linked to gender? Consider Marla Ludvik's conduct in showing others the photographs of Burns: would Burns have to prove that Ludvik would not have displayed nude photographs of a male worker whom she disliked? Or was it the sexualized nature of the insult that made that an act of sex discrimination? Should that count as sex discrimination?

3. *Flaws in the Theory.* Professor Vicki Schultz criticizes sexual harassment case law for under-inclusiveness. She argues that courts have conflated gender and sexual abuse, by too often presuming that the latter indicated and was necessary for the former. As a result, the law misses much of the worst harassment of women, because it isn't sexual. Gender-based, non-sexual insults ("you don't look like a mechanic") undermine women's competence and authority. What they have in common with sexualized harassment such as that in *Burns*, Schultz argues, is that the victim's very womanness is used as evidence of her inadequacy. It is also, she says, overinclusive, because judges often tend to assume that any sexualized conduct or speech is discriminatory. Vicki Schultz, "Reconceptualizing Sexual Harassment," 107 *Yale L. J.* 1683 (1998).

Page 930—Substitute the following for the *McWilliams* case and the Notes following it:

Joseph Oncale v. Sundowner Offshore Services, Inc., et al.

United States Supreme Court, 1998.
523 U.S. ___, 118 S.Ct. 998, 140 L.Ed.2d 201.

■ JUSTICE SCALIA delivered the opinion of the Court.

This case presents the question whether workplace harassment can violate Title VII's prohibition against "discriminat[ion] ... because of ... sex," 42 U.S.C. § 2000e–2(a)(1), when the harasser and the harassed employee are of the same sex.

The District Court having granted summary judgment for respondent, we must assume the facts to be as alleged by petitioner Joseph Oncale. The precise details are irrelevant to the legal point we must decide, and in the interest of both brevity and dignity we shall describe them only generally. In late October 1991, Oncale was working for respondent Sundowner Offshore Services on a Chevron U.S. A., Inc., oil platform in the Gulf of Mexico. He was employed as a roustabout on an eight-man crew which included respondents John Lyons, Danny Pippen, and Brandon Johnson. Lyons, the crane operator, and Pippen, the driller, had supervisory authority. On several occasions, Oncale was forcibly subjected to sex-related, humiliating actions against him by Lyons, Pippen and Johnson in the presence of the rest of the crew. Pippen and Lyons also physically assaulted Oncale in a sexual manner, and Lyons threatened him with rape.

Oncale's complaints to supervisory personnel produced no remedial action; in fact, the company's Safety Compliance Clerk, Valent Hohen, told Oncale that Lyons and Pippen "picked [on] him all the time too," and called him a name suggesting homosexuality. Oncale eventually quit— asking that his pink slip reflect that he "voluntarily left due to sexual harassment and verbal abuse." When asked at his deposition why he left Sundowner, Oncale stated "I felt that if I didn't leave my job, that I would be raped or forced to have sex."

Oncale filed a complaint against Sundowner in the United States District Court for the Eastern District of Louisiana, alleging that he was discriminated against in his employment because of his sex. Relying on the Fifth Circuit's decision in *Garcia v. Elf Atochem North America,* 28 F.3d 446, 451–452 (C.A.5 1994), the district court held that "Mr. Oncale, a male, has no cause of action under Title VII for harassment by male co-workers." On appeal, a panel of the Fifth Circuit concluded that *Garcia* was binding Circuit precedent, and affirmed. 83 F.3d 118 (1996). We granted certiorari.

Title VII of the Civil Rights Act of 1964 provides, in relevant part, that "[i]t shall be an unlawful employment practice for an employer * * * to discriminate against any individual with respect to his compensation, terms, conditions, or privileges of employment, because of such individual's race, color, religion, sex, or national origin." 78 Stat. 255, as amended, 42 U.S.C. § 2000e–2(a)(1). We have held that this not only covers "terms" and "conditions" in the narrow contractual sense, but "evinces a congressional intent to strike at the entire spectrum of disparate treatment of men and women in employment." *Meritor Savings Bank, FSB v. Vinson*, 477 U.S. 57, 64 (1986) (citations and internal quotation marks omitted). "When the workplace is permeated with discriminatory intimidation, ridicule, and insult that is sufficiently severe or pervasive to alter the conditions of the victim's employment and create an abusive working environment, Title VII is violated." *Harris v. Forklift Systems, Inc.*, 510 U.S. 17, 21 (1993) (citations and internal quotation marks omitted).

Title VII's prohibition of discrimination "because of ... sex" protects men as well as women, *Newport News Shipbuilding & Dry Dock Co. v. EEOC*, 462 U.S. 669, 682 (1983), and in the related context of racial discrimination in the workplace we have rejected any conclusive presumption that an employer will not discriminate against members of his own race. "Because of the many facets of human motivation, it would be unwise to presume as a matter of law that human beings of one definable group will not discriminate against other members of that group." *Castaneda v. Partida*, 430 U.S. 482, 499 (1977). In *Johnson v. Transportation Agency, Santa Clara Cty.*, 480 U.S. 616 (1987), a male employee claimed that his employer discriminated against him because of his sex when it preferred a female employee for promotion. Although we ultimately rejected the claim on other grounds, we did not consider it significant that the supervisor who made that decision was also a man. If our precedents leave any doubt on the question, we hold today that nothing in Title VII necessarily bars a claim of discrimination "because of ... sex" merely because the plaintiff and the defendant (or the person charged with acting on behalf of the defendant) are of the same sex.

Courts have had little trouble with that principle in cases like *Johnson*, where an employee claims to have been passed over for a job or promotion. But when the issue arises in the context of a "hostile environment" sexual harassment claim, the state and federal courts have taken a bewildering variety of stances. Some, like the Fifth Circuit in this case, have held that same-sex sexual harassment claims are never cognizable under Title VII. See also, e.g., *Goluszek v. H.P. Smith*, 697 F.Supp. 1452 (N.D.Ill.1988). Other decisions say that such claims are actionable only if the plaintiff can prove that the harasser is homosexual (and thus presumably motivated by sexual desire). Compare *McWilliams v. Fairfax County Board of Supervisors*, 72 F.3d 1191 (C.A.4 1996), with *Wrightson v. Pizza Hut of America*, 99 F.3d 138 (C.A.4 1996). Still others suggest that workplace harassment that is sexual in content is always actionable, regardless of the harasser's sex, sexual orientation, or motivations. See *Doe v. Belleville*, 119 F.3d 563 (C.A.7 1997).

We see no justification in the statutory language or our precedents for a categorical rule excluding same-sex harassment claims from the coverage of Title VII. As some courts have observed, male-on-male sexual harassment in the workplace was assuredly not the principal evil Congress was concerned with when it enacted Title VII. But statutory prohibitions often go beyond the principal evil to cover reasonably comparable evils, and it is ultimately the provisions of our laws rather than the principal concerns of our legislators by which we are governed. Title VII prohibits "discriminat[ion] . . . because of . . . sex" in the "terms" or "conditions" of employment. Our holding that this includes sexual harassment must extend to sexual harassment of any kind that meets the statutory requirements.

Respondents and their amici contend that recognizing liability for same-sex harassment will transform Title VII into a general civility code for the American workplace. But that risk is no greater for same-sex than for opposite-sex harassment, and is adequately met by careful attention to the requirements of the statute. Title VII does not prohibit all verbal or physical harassment in the workplace; it is directed only at "discriminat[ion] . . . because of . . . sex." We have never held that workplace harassment, even harassment between men and women, is automatically discrimination because of sex merely because the words used have sexual content or connotations. "The critical issue, Title VII's text indicates, is whether members of one sex are exposed to disadvantageous terms or conditions of employment to which members of the other sex are not exposed." *Harris, supra,* at 25 (Ginsburg, J., concurring).

Courts and juries have found the inference of discrimination easy to draw in most male-female sexual harassment situations, because the challenged conduct typically involves explicit or implicit proposals of sexual activity; it is reasonable to assume those proposals would not have been made to someone of the same sex. The same chain of inference would be available to a plaintiff alleging same-sex harassment, if there were credible evidence that the harasser was homosexual. But harassing conduct need not be motivated by sexual desire to support an inference of discrimination on the basis of sex. A trier of fact might reasonably find such discrimination, for example, if a female victim is harassed in such sex-specific and derogatory terms by another woman as to make it clear that the harasser is motivated by general hostility to the presence of women in the workplace. A same-sex harassment plaintiff may also, of course, offer direct comparative evidence about how the alleged harasser treated members of both sexes in a mixed-sex workplace. Whatever evidentiary route the plaintiff chooses to follow, he or she must always prove that the conduct at issue was not merely tinged with offensive sexual connotations, but actually constituted "discrimina[tion] . . . because of . . . sex."

And there is another requirement that prevents Title VII from expanding into a general civility code: As we emphasized in *Meritor* and *Harris,* the statute does not reach genuine but innocuous differences in the ways men and women routinely interact with members of the same sex and of the opposite sex. The prohibition of harassment on the basis of sex requires neither asexuality nor androgyny in the workplace; it forbids only behavior so objectively offensive as to alter the "conditions" of the victim's employment. "Conduct that is not severe or pervasive enough to create an objectively hostile or abusive work environment—an environment that a reasonable person would find hostile or abusive—is beyond Title VII's purview." *Harris*, 510 U.S., at 21, citing *Meritor*, 477 U.S., at 67. We have always regarded that requirement as crucial, and as sufficient to ensure that courts and juries do not mistake ordinary socializing in the workplace—such as male-on-male horseplay or intersexual flirtation—for discriminatory "conditions of employment."

We have emphasized, moreover, that the objective severity of harassment should be judged from the perspective of a reasonable person in the plaintiff's position, considering "all the circumstances." *Harris, supra*, at 23. In same-sex (as in all) harassment cases, that inquiry requires careful consideration of the social context in which particular behavior occurs and is experienced by its target. A professional football player's working environment is not severely or pervasively abusive, for example, if the coach smacks him on the buttocks as he heads onto the field—even if the same behavior would reasonably be experienced as abusive by the coach's secretary (male or female) back at the office. The real social impact of workplace behavior often depends on a constellation of surrounding circumstances, expectations, and relationships which are not fully captured by a simple recitation of the words used or the physical acts performed. Common sense, and an appropriate sensitivity to social context, will enable courts and juries to distinguish between simple teasing or roughhousing among members of the same sex, and conduct which a reasonable person in the plaintiff's position would find severely hostile or abusive.

Because we conclude that sex discrimination consisting of same-sex sexual harassment is actionable under Title VII, the judgment of the Court of Appeals for the Fifth Circuit is reversed, and the case is remanded for further proceedings consistent with this opinion.

■ JUSTICE THOMAS, Concurring.

I concur because the Court stresses that in every sexual harassment case, the plaintiff must plead and ultimately prove Title VII's statutory requirement that there be discrimination "because of . . . sex."

NOTES ON SAME–SEX HARASSMENT

1. *What Next?* The Court rules that same-sex harassment claims are not prohibited as a matter of law. But how will a plaintiff like Oncale prove that the sexually assaultive conduct fell within the "because of . . . sex" requirement? The Court declines to describe the conduct, which included other men placing their penises on Oncale's body and one incident in which a bar of soap was forced into his rectum. See the Fifth Circuit opinion at 83 F.3d at 118–119. At trial, what will Oncale's theory of the case be? Remember that the oil rig where Oncale worked had an all-male workforce. How will he prove differential treatment?

2. *Could It Be Gender?* The *Dillon* court distinguished *Price Waterhouse v. Hopkins* in part because it found that the co-workers who called Dillon a "fag" were not relying on sexual stereotypes. Other courts, however, have ruled that actions such as calling a man "fag" or "queer" and harassing him for wearing an earring reflect stereotypical ideas about how men and women should behave or appear. The Court vacated and remanded one such decision for further consideration in light of *Oncale. Doe v. City of Belleville*, 119 F.3d 563 (7th Cir.1997), *vacated and remanded*, 118 S.Ct. 1183 (1998). Note that the word "gender" does not appear even once in the *Oncale* opinion. For an excellent analysis of gender in the context of same-sex harassment law, see Katherine Franke, *What's Wrong With Sexual Harassment?*, 49 Stan.L.Rev. 691 (1997).

3. *"Common Sense"?* The final portion of the opinion exhorts lower courts not to confuse "ordinary socializing in the workplace–such as male-on-male horseplay or intersexual flirtation" with harassment. Does that suggest that the bounds of what is inoffensive horseplay are determined by gender? If so, how can a court require a showing of differential treatment? Isn't differential treatment built into the very distinction between horseplay and harassment?

4. *The Role of Sexual Orientation.* The Court states that one way to prove discrimination would be to offer "credible evidence that the harasser was homosexual." How will discovery proceed in such cases, especially if the harasser denies he is homosexual? What definition will a trial judge use for "homosexual"? See the description of "stereotypical homosexual behavior" in *Griswold v. Fresenius USA, Inc.*, 978 F.Supp. 718, 723–4 (N.D.Ohio 1997). Will bisexuality count? Doesn't this chain of inference mean that heterosexuals will be allowed to engage in the same acts for which homosexuals will be held liable? Compare the facts of *McWilliams* to *Wrightson v. Pizza Hut of America, Inc.*, 99 F.3d 138 (4th Cir.1996), where the court found that gay men had harassed a heterosexual man.

5. *Sexual Orientation and "Common Sense."* Whose sensibilities will establish the reasonable person standard for severity or unwelcomeness when the alleged harasser is gay and the plaintiff is straight? Do you think that the Court's use of "intersexual" to modify "flirtation" was intended as a specific limit, to guard against a man being allowed to flirt with another man, or a woman with another woman? Justice Scalia uses the example of a professional football coach patting a player on the buttocks to illustrate harmless behavior. What if the coach is gay? One court has stated that it "cannot rule out that the homosexual aspect of harassment could objectively contribute to a hostile environment." *Miller v. Vesta, Inc.*, 946 F.Supp. 697, 712–3 (E.D.Wis.1996).

6. *Distinguishing Sex and Sexual Orientation.* Review Note 7 on page 935 of the casebook. After *Oncale,* each should withstand a motion to dismiss. What would your theory of the case be for each?

7. *State Law and Same–Sex Harassment.* In six states, courts have ruled that allegations of same-sex harassment state a cause of action for sex discrimination under the state anti-discrimination statute. *Storey v. Chase Bankcard Services, Inc.,* 970 F.Supp. 722 (D.Ariz.1997) (interpreting Arizona law); *Fiol v. Doellstedt,* 50 Cal.App.4th 1318, 58 Cal.Rptr.2d 308 (2d Dist.1996); *Melnychenko v. 84 Lumber Co.,* 424 Mass. 285, 676 N.E.2d 45 (Mass. 1997); *Cummings v. Koehnen,* 568 N.W.2d 418 (Minn.1997); *Zalewski v. Overlook Hospital,* 300 N.J.Super. 202, 692 A.2d 131 (1996), citing *Lehmann v. Toys 'R' Us,* 132 N.J. 587, 626 A.2d 445 (N.J. 1993); and *Tarver v. Calex Corp.,* 1998 WL 74378 (Ohio Ct.App.1998) (unpublished).

3.   CURRENT ISSUES IN WORKPLACE DISCRIMINATION

PART B.   LEGAL BANS AGAINST SEXUAL ORIENTATION DISCRIMINATION

Page 957–Add the following at the end of *Ross*:

City of Atlanta v. Morgan

Supreme Court of Georgia, 1997.
268 Ga. 586, 492 S.E.2d 193.

■ JUSTICE HUNSTEIN.

* * * Atlanta [] City Ordinance 96–O–1018 [] provides certain insurance benefits for dependents of City of Atlanta employees who qualify and are registered as domestic partners. * * * This benefits ordinance was enacted in response to our opinion in *City of Atlanta v. McKinney,* 265 Ga. 161, 454 S.E.2d 517 (1995), in which we upheld the constitutionality of the registry[] but held unconstitutional the City's original benefit's ordinance (Ordinance 93–O–1057) because in it the City had recognized domestic partnerships as "a family relationship" and provided employee benefits to domestic partners "in a comparable manner . . . as for a spouse," thereby expanding the definition of "dependent" in a manner inconsistent with State law and in violation of both the Georgia Constitution and OCGA § 36–35–6(b). The issue in *McKinney,* as in this appeal, was whether the City acted within its authority to provide benefits to its employees and their dependents by defining "dependent" consistent with State law.

OCGA § 36–35–4(a) authorizes a municipality to provide insurance benefits to its employees and their dependents. Although this section of the Municipal Home Rule Act grants specific authority to provide such benefits to the dependents of a municipal employee, it does not provide a definition of the term "dependent." In order to determine whether the definition provided in the City's benefits ordinance is consistent with State law, we must, therefore, look to the ordinary meaning of the term as well as the way in which it is defined in other statutes.

The City's benefits ordinance defines a "dependent" as "one who relies on another for financial support" and provides that an employee's domestic partner shall be dependent if:

(i) The employee makes contributions to the domestic partner of cash and supplies, and the domestic partner relies upon and uses those contributions to support himself/herself in order to maintain his or her standard of living. The contributions may be at irregular intervals and of irregular amounts, but must have existed for at least six months, and must be continuing.

(ii) The employee is obligated, based upon his/her commitment set forth in the Declaration of Domestic Partnership, to continue the financial support of the domestic partner for so long as the domestic partnership shall be in effect.

(iii) The domestic partner is supported, in whole or in part, by the employee's earnings, and has been for at least the last six months. Ordinance 96–O–1018 (a)(1)(B).

Based on our review of other definitions of "dependent" in Georgia case law, we conclude that the ordinance's definition of "dependent" is consistent with both the common, ordinary meaning of the term "dependent" and the definition attributed to that term as it is used in the Georgia statutes. * * *

Postscript. One of the attorneys for the City of Atlanta who successfully defended the partner benefits ordinance was Robin Shahar.

Page 957—Add to Note 1:

Domestic partner benefits have also been extended to public sector employees in Hawaii, by the Hawaii Reciprocal Beneficiaries Act (RBA), enacted in 1997. The Act purports to cover all workers in the state, but state officials entered into a consent judgment agreeing that employers whose benefits plans are governed by federal law are exempt from the RBA. See new Note 4, *infra.* [See Chapter 9 of this Supplement, p. 111.] Also new since the casebook was published are domestic partner benefits laws in Philadelphia and New York City.

Update on San Francisco and Catholic Charities—The anticipated lawsuit described in the text did not materialize. Instead, Catholic Charities opted to extend benefits to any one person living in an employee's household whom the employee designated. In this way, the extension of benefits is not limited to unmarried or gay partners and no "recognition" of such relationships is necessary.

Page 958—Add to Note 2:

The Alaska Supreme Court found that denial of health benefits to domestic partners of state university employees violated that state's prohibition against marital status discrimination, but during the pendency of the case, the state legislature amended the benefits law to specify that limiting benefits to spouses would not violate the civil rights statute. *University of Alaska v. Tumeo*, 933 P.2d 1147 (Alaska 1997). In a similar case, a New Jersey appeals court found that the marital status distinction was justified by the state's rational interest in "creating a workable administrative scheme" for its benefits program. *Rutgers Council of AAUP Chapters v. Rutgers*, 689 A.2d 828, 833 (N.J.Super.1997). Concurring Judge Paul G. Levy, noting that the result was "distasteful," added, "I also commend to the Legislature its examination of the marriage laws to consider the creation of legal responsibilities between domestic partners, both homosexual as well as heterosexual, perhaps based on objective criteria to permit registration of a domestic partnership as is recognized in New York City* * *." *Id.* at 466–7, 840.

Page 958–Add new Notes 4 and 5:

4. *Federal Law Complications.* In both *Ross* and *Phillips*, *supra*, the plaintiffs were employees of the state government. Private sector employers who offer a health benefits plan are governed by a federal statute, the Employee Retirement Income Security Act (ERISA), 29 U.S.C. SS 1001 *et seq.* (State and federal government employers are not covered by ERISA.) ERISA has a broad pre-emption clause, which has been interpreted to prohibit the enforcement of any state laws mandating particular health benefits against employers covered by ERISA. *See, Metropolitan Life Ins. Co. v. Massachusetts*, 471 U.S. 724 (1985). Under ERISA, employers are not barred from voluntarily offering domestic partner benefits [see p. 794 of text], but they cannot be ordered by a state statute to do so.

A group of airlines and other employers covered by ERISA challenged the San Francisco ordinance described in Note 1 in the text, as violating federal law. In determining whether the city was ordering the companies to comply in a regulatory capacity (in which case ERISA pre-emption would apply), or merely acting as a "market participant" seeking contractors for outsourcing work by contract (in which case it wouldn't), the court analyzed the role that the city plays vis-a-vis these businesses. The court ruled that because the city as a monopoly controlled the airport, it was acting as a regulator. Thus, citing ERISA, the court enjoined the application of the ordinance, insofar as it concerns health benefits, against those plaintiffs. The court reasoned that denying city contracts to businesses not offering domestic partner coverage was of sufficient impact that it amounted to regulation, or, in essence, a mandated benefit. However, application of the ordinance as to benefits not covered by ERISA (free travel, e.g.), was not pre-empted. *Air Transport Ass'n of America v. City and County of San Francisco*, 992 F. Supp. 1149 (N.D.Ca.1998).

An additional complication of the San Francisco ordinance was its application to large companies with employees outside as well as inside the city limits of San Francisco. The court ruled that forcing such employers to extend partner benefits to workers outside the city who were not working on city contracts violated what is known as the "dormant" Commerce Clause. Because regulation of interstate commerce lies within the sole province of Congress, the city was barred from imposing economic regulations except on employer-employee relationships located in the city or in situations where the work being performed was pursuant to a city contract. *Id.*

PART C.   AIDS IN THE WORKPLACE

Page 963–Insert prior to the *Anderson* decision:

Randon Bragdon, v. Sidney Abbott, et al.

United States Supreme Court, 1998.
___ U.S. ___, 118 S.Ct. 2196, ___ L.Ed.2d ___.

■ JUSTICE KENNEDY delivered the opinion of the Court.

We address in this case the application of the Americans with Disabilities Act of 1990 (ADA), 104 Stat. 327, 42 U.S.C. § 12101 et seq., to persons infected with the human immunodeficiency virus (HIV). We granted certiorari to review, first, whether HIV infection is a disability under the ADA when the infection has not yet progressed to the so-called symptomatic phase; and, second, whether the Court of Appeals, in affirming a grant of summary judgment, cited sufficient material in the record to determine, as a matter of law, that respondent's infection with HIV posed no direct threat to the health and safety of her treating dentist.

I

Respondent Sidney Abbott has been infected with HIV since 1986. When the incidents we recite occurred, her infection had not manifested its most serious symptoms. On September 16, 1994, she went to the office of petitioner Randon Bragdon in Bangor, Maine, for a dental appointment. She disclosed her HIV infection on the patient registration form. Petitioner completed a dental examination, discovered a cavity, and informed respondent of his policy against filling cavities of HIV-infected patients. He offered to perform the work at a hospital with no added fee for his services, though respondent would be responsible for the cost of using the hospital's facilities. Respondent declined.

Respondent sued petitioner under state law and § 302 of the ADA, 104 Stat. 355, 42 U.S.C. § 12182, alleging discrimination on the basis of her disability. The state law claims are not before us. Section 302 of the ADA provides:

"No individual shall be discriminated against on the basis of disability in the full and equal enjoyment of the goods, services, facilities, privileges, advantages, or accommodations of any place of public accommodation by any person who . . . operates a place of public accommodation." § 12182(a).

The term "public accommodation" is defined to include the "professional office of a health care provider." § 12181(7)(F).

A later subsection qualifies the mandate not to discriminate. It provides:

"Nothing in this subchapter shall require an entity to permit an individual to participate in or benefit from the goods, services, facilities, privileges, advantages and accommodations of such entity where such individual poses a direct threat to the health or safety of others." § 12182(b)(3). * * *

II

We first review the ruling that respondent's HIV infection constituted a disability under the ADA. The statute defines disability as:

"(A) a physical or mental impairment that substantially limits one or more of the major life activities of such individual;

"(B) a record of such an impairment; or

"(C) being regarded as having such impairment." § 12102(2).

We hold respondent's HIV infection was a disability under subsection (A) of the definitional section of the statute. In light of this conclusion, we need not consider the applicability of subsections (B) or (C).

Our consideration of subsection (A) of the definition proceeds in three steps. First, we consider whether respondent's HIV infection was a physical impairment. Second, we identify the life activity upon which respondent relies (reproduction and child bearing) and determine whether it constitutes a major life activity under the ADA. Third, tying the two statutory phrases together, we ask whether the impairment substantially limited the major life activity. In construing the statute, we are informed by interpretations of parallel definitions in previous statutes and the views of various administrative agencies which have faced this interpretive question.

A

The ADA's definition of disability is drawn almost verbatim from the definition of "handicapped individual" included in the Rehabilitation Act of 1973, 29 U.S.C. § 706(8)(B) (1988 ed.), and the definition of "handicap" contained in the Fair Housing Amendments Act of 1988, 42 U.S.C. § 3602(h)(1) (1988 ed.). Congress' repetition of a well-established term carries the implication that Congress intended the term to be construed in accordance with pre-existing regulatory interpretations. In this case, Congress did more than suggest this construction; it adopted a specific statutory provision in the ADA directing as follows:

> "Except as otherwise provided in this chapter, nothing in this chapter shall be construed to apply a lesser standard than the standards applied under title V of the Rehabilitation Act of 1973 (29 U.S.C. 790 et seq.) or the regulations issued by Federal agencies pursuant to such title." 42 U.S.C. § 12201(a).

The directive requires us to construe the ADA to grant at least as much protection as provided by the regulations implementing the Rehabilitation Act.

1

The first step in the inquiry under subsection (A) requires us to determine whether respondent's condition constituted a physical impairment. The Department of Health, Education and Welfare (HEW) issued the first regulations interpreting the Rehabilitation Act in 1977. The regulations are of particular significance because, at the time, HEW was the agency responsible for coordinating the implementation and enforcement of § 504. The HEW regulations, which appear without change in the current regulations issued by the Department of Health and Human Services, define "physical or mental impairment" to mean:

> "(A) any physiological disorder or condition, cosmetic disfigurement, or anatomical loss affecting one or more of the following body systems: neurological; musculoskeletal; special sense organs; respiratory, including speech organs; cardiovascular; reproductive, digestive, genito-urinary; hemic and lymphatic; skin; and endocrine; or

> "(B) any mental or psychological disorder, such as mental retardation, organic brain syndrome, emotional or mental illness, and specific learning disabilities." 45 CFR § 84.3(j)(2)(i) (1997).

In issuing these regulations, HEW decided against including a list of disorders constituting physical or mental impairments, out of concern that any specific enumeration might not be comprehensive. 42 Fed.Reg. 22685 (1977), reprinted in 45 CFR pt. 84, App. A, p. 334 (1997). The commentary accompanying the regulations, however, contains a representative list of disorders and conditions constituting physical impairments, including "such diseases and conditions as orthopedic, visual, speech, and hearing impairments, cerebral palsy, epilepsy, muscular dystrophy, multiple sclerosis, cancer, heart disease, diabetes, mental retardation, emotional illness, and ... drug addiction and alcoholism." Ibid.

* * * HIV infection is not included in the list of specific disorders constituting physical impairments, in part because HIV was not identified as the cause of AIDS until 1983. * * *

The disease follows a predictable and, as of today, an unalterable course. Once a person is infected with HIV, the virus invades different cells in the blood and in body tissues. Certain white blood cells, known as helper T-lymphocytes or CD4+ cells, are particularly vulnerable to HIV. The virus attaches to the CD4 receptor site of the target cell and fuses its membrane to the cell's membrane. HIV is a retrovirus, which means it uses an enzyme to convert its own genetic material into a form indistinguishable from the genetic material of the target cell. The virus' genetic material migrates to the cell's nucleus and becomes integrated with the cell's chromosomes. Once integrated, the virus can use the cell's own genetic machinery to replicate itself. Additional copies of the virus are released into the body and infect other cells in turn. * * * The virus eventually kills the infected host cell. * * *

[The Court then summarized the three stages of HIV infection, from the acute or primary stage typically lasting three months after infection occurs; to a period of less acute symptoms, known as the asymptomatic stage (which the Court calls "a misnomer"), typically lasting 7 to 11 years; and finally to a formal diagnosis of AIDS, when the CD4 cells drop below a minimal number.]

In light of the immediacy with which the virus begins to damage the infected person's white blood cells and the severity of the disease, we hold it is an impairment from the moment of infection. As noted earlier, infection with HIV causes immediate abnormalities in a person's blood, and the infected person's white cell count continues to drop throughout the course of the disease, even when the attack is concentrated in the lymph nodes. In light of these facts, HIV infection must be regarded as a physiological disorder with a constant and detrimental effect on the infected person's hemic and lymphatic systems from the moment of infection. HIV infection satisfies the statutory and regulatory definition of a physical impairment during every stage of the disease.

2

The statute is not operative, and the definition not satisfied, unless the impairment affects a major life activity. Respondent's claim throughout this case has been that the HIV infection placed a substantial limitation on her ability to reproduce and to bear children. Given the pervasive, and invariably fatal, course of the disease, its effect on major life activities of many sorts might have been relevant to our inquiry. Respondent and a number of amici make arguments about HIV's profound impact on almost every phase of the infected person's life. In light of these submissions, it may seem legalistic to circumscribe our discussion to the activity of reproduction. We have little doubt that had different parties brought the suit they would have maintained that an HIV infection imposes substantial limitations on other major life activities.

From the outset, however, the case has been treated as one in which reproduction was the major life activity limited by the impairment. It is our practice to decide cases on the grounds raised and considered in the Court of Appeals and included in the question on which we granted certiorari. We ask, then, whether reproduction is a major life activity.

We have little difficulty concluding that it is. As the Court of Appeals held, "[t]he plain meaning of the word 'major' denotes comparative importance" and "suggest[s] that the touchstone for determining an activity's inclusion under the statutory rubric is its significance." 107 F.3d, at 939, 940. Reproduction falls well within the phrase "major life activity." Reproduction and the sexual dynamics surrounding it are central to the life process itself.

While petitioner concedes the importance of reproduction, he claims that Congress intended the ADA only to cover those aspects of a person's life which have a public, economic, or daily character. The argument founders on the statutory language. Nothing in the definition suggests that activities without a public, economic, or daily dimension may somehow be regarded as so unimportant or insignificant as to fall outside the meaning of the word "major." The breadth of the term confounds the attempt to limit its construction in this manner.

* * * The[] regulations [under the Rehabilitation Act] are contrary to petitioner's attempt to limit the meaning of the term "major" to public activities. The inclusion of activities such as caring for one's self and performing manual tasks belies the suggestion that a task must have a public or economic character in order to be a major life activity for purposes of the ADA. On the contrary, the Rehabilitation Act regulations support the inclusion of reproduction as a major life activity, since reproduction could not be regarded as any less important than working and learning. Petitioner advances no credible basis for confining major life activities to those with a public, economic, or daily aspect. In the absence of any reason to reach a contrary conclusion, we agree with the Court of Appeals' determination that reproduction is a major life activity for the purposes of the ADA.

3

The final element of the disability definition in subsection (A) is whether respondent's physical impairment was a substantial limit on the major life activity she asserts. * * *

Our evaluation of the medical evidence leads us to conclude that respondent's infection substantially limited her ability to reproduce in two independent ways. First, a woman infected with HIV who tries to conceive a child imposes on the man a significant risk of becoming infected. The cumulative results of 13 studies collected in a 1994 textbook on AIDS indicates that 20% of male partners of women with HIV became HIV-positive themselves, with a majority of the studies finding a statistically significant risk of infection.

Second, an infected woman risks infecting her child during gestation and childbirth, i.e., perinatal transmission. Petitioner concedes that women infected with HIV face about a 25% risk of transmitting the virus to their children. Published reports available in 1994 confirm the accuracy of this statistic.

Petitioner points to evidence in the record suggesting that antiretroviral therapy can lower the risk of perinatal transmission to about 8%. * * * It cannot be said as a matter of law that an 8% risk of transmitting a dread and fatal disease to one's child does not represent a substantial limitation on reproduction.

The Act addresses substantial limitations on major life activities, not utter inabilities. Conception and childbirth are not impossible for an HIV victim but, without doubt, are dangerous to the public health. This meets the definition of a substantial limitation. The decision to reproduce carries economic and legal consequences as well. There are added costs for antiretroviral therapy, supplemental insurance, and long-term health care for the child who must be examined and, tragic to think, treated for the infection. The laws of some States, moreover, forbid persons infected with HIV from having sex with others, regardless of consent.

In the end, the disability definition does not turn on personal choice. When significant limitations result from the impairment, the definition is met even if the difficulties are not insurmountable. For the statistical and other reasons we have cited, of course, the limitations on reproduction may be insurmountable here. Testimony from the respondent that her HIV infection controlled her decision not to have a child is unchallenged. In the context of reviewing summary judgment, we must take it to be true. We agree with the District Court and the Court of Appeals that no triable issue of fact impedes a ruling on the question of statutory coverage. Respondent's HIV infection is a physical impairment which substantially limits a major life activity, as the ADA defines it. In view of our holding, we need not address the second question presented, i.e., whether HIV infection is a per se disability under the ADA.

[The Court described the interpretation of the definition under the Rehabilitation Act and found a "uniformity of the administrative and judicial precedent construing the definition" in agreement with its conclusion *supra*. It concluded that Congress was aware of such precedent when enacting the ADA "and intended to give that position its active endorsement." The Court then reviewed the administrative guidance issued by the Department of Justice and the EEOC under the ADA itself and again found uniformity on the point that asymptomatic HIV infection constituted a disability within the meaning of the ADA.]

III

* * * Notwithstanding the protection given respondent by the ADA's definition of disability, petitioner could have refused to treat her if her infectious condition "pose[d] a direct threat to the health or safety of others." 42 U.S.C. § 12182(b)(3). The ADA defines a direct threat to be "a significant risk to the health or safety of others that cannot be eliminated by a modification of policies, practices, or procedures or by the provision of auxiliary aids or services." *Ibid.* Parallel provisions appear in the employment provisions of Title I. §§ 12111(3), 12113(b).

The ADA's direct threat provision stems from the recognition in *School Bd. of Nassau Cty. v. Arline,* 480 U.S. 273, 287 (1987), of the importance of prohibiting discrimination against individuals with disabilities while protecting others from significant health and safety risks, resulting, for instance, from a contagious disease. In *Arline,* the Court reconciled these objectives by construing the Rehabilitation Act not to require the hiring of a person who posed "a significant risk of communicating an infectious disease to others." *Id.,* at 287, n.16. Congress amended the Rehabilitation Act and the Fair Housing Act to incorporate the language. See 29 U.S.C. § 706(8)(D) (excluding individuals who "would constitute a direct threat to the health or safety of other individuals"); 42 U.S.C. § 3604(f)(9) (same). It later relied on the same language in enacting the ADA. See 28 CFR pt. 36, App. B, p. 626 (1997) (ADA's direct threat provision codifies *Arline*). Because few, if any, activities in life are risk free, *Arline* and the ADA do not ask whether a risk exists, but whether it is significant.

The existence, or nonexistence, of a significant risk must be determined from the standpoint of the person who refuses the treatment or accommodation, and the risk assessment must be based on medical or other objective evidence. As a health care professional, petitioner had the duty to assess the risk of infection based on the objective, scientific information available to him and others in his profession. His belief that a significant risk existed, even if maintained in good faith, would not relieve him from liability. * * * [P]etitioner receives no special deference simply because he is a health care professional. It is true that *Arline* reserved "the question whether courts should also defer to the reasonable medical judgments of private physicians on which an employer has relied." 480 U.S., at 288, n. 18. At most, this statement reserved the possibility that employers could consult with individual physicians as objective third-party experts. It did not suggest that an individual physician's state of mind could excuse discrimination without regard to the objective reasonableness of his actions.

Our conclusion that courts should assess the objective reasonableness of the views of health care professionals without deferring to their individual judgments does not answer * * * whether petitioner's actions were reasonable in light of the available medical evidence. In assessing the reasonableness of petitioner's actions, the views of public health authorities, such as the U.S. Public Health Service, CDC, and the National Institutes of Health, are of special weight and authority. The views of these organizations are not conclusive, however. A health care professional who disagrees with the prevailing medical consensus may refute it by citing a credible scientific basis for deviating from the accepted norm.

[The Court reviewed the scientific evidence in the record and found that the court of appeals had properly weighed much of it before granting summary judgment for the plaintiff. The Court was concerned, however, that the appeals court had improperly inferred from the CDC Dentistry Guidelines on reduction of risk that following such guidelines rendered the treatment of HIV-infected patients safe, which the Guidelines did not explicitly say. The Court also questioned whether the appeals court gave too much weight to a policy statement from the American Dental Association, which is not a public health agency. Finally, the Court questioned whether the data available at the time defendant denied treatment to the plaintiff in his office as to possible workplace transmission to seven dental workers "might have provided some, albeit not necessarily sufficient, support" for his position. However, "we have not had briefs and arguments directed to the entire record." The Court therefore remanded to the court of appeals to "permit a full exploration of the issue through the adversary process."]

■ [The concurring opinions of JUSTICE BREYER, joined by JUSTICE STEVENS, and of JUSTICE GINSBURG, are omitted.]

■ CHIEF JUSTICE REHNQUIST, with whom JUSTICE SCALIA, and JUSTICE THOMAS join, and with whom JUSTICE O'CONNOR joins as to Part II, concurring in the judgment in part and dissenting in part.

I

* * * Petitioner does not dispute that asymptomatic HIV-positive status is a physical impairment. I therefore assume this to be the case, and proceed to the second and third statutory requirements for "disability."

According to the Court, the next question is "whether reproduction is a major life activity." That, however, is only half of the relevant question. As mentioned above, the ADA's definition of a "disability" requires that the major life activity at issue be one "of such individual." § 12102(2)(A). The Court truncates the question, perhaps because there is not a shred of record evidence indicating that, prior to becoming infected with HIV, respondent's major life activities included reproduction[4] (assuming for the moment that reproduction is a major life activity at all). At most, the record indicates that after learning of her HIV status, respondent, whatever her previous inclination, conclusively decided that she would not have

---

4. * * * I assume that in using the term reproduction, respondent and the Court are referring to the numerous discrete activities that comprise the reproductive process, and that is the sense in which I have used the term.

children. There is absolutely no evidence that, absent the HIV, respondent would have had or was even considering having children. Indeed, when asked during her deposition whether her HIV infection had in any way impaired her ability to carry out any of her life functions, respondent answered "No." It is further telling that in the course of her entire brief to this Court, respondent studiously avoids asserting even once that reproduction is a major life activity to her. To the contrary, she argues that the "major life activity" inquiry should not turn on a particularized assessment of the circumstances of this or any other case.

But even aside from the facts of this particular case, the Court is simply wrong in concluding as a general matter that reproduction is a "major life activity." * * * [T]he Court argues that reproduction is a "major" life activity in that it is "central to the life process itself." In support of this reading, the Court focuses on the fact that " 'major' " indicates " 'comparative importance,' "; see also Webster's Collegiate Dictionary 702 (10th ed.1994) ("greater in dignity, rank, importance, or interest"), ignoring the alternative definition of "major" as "greater in quantity, number, or extent." It is the latter definition that is most consistent with the ADA's illustrative list of major life activities.

No one can deny that reproductive decisions are important in a person's life. But so are decisions as to who[m] to marry, where to live, and how to earn one's living. Fundamental importance of this sort is not the common thread linking the statute's listed activities. The common thread is rather that the activities are repetitively performed and essential in the day-to-day existence of a normally functioning individual. They are thus quite different from the series of activities leading to the birth of a child.

* * * But even if I were to assume that reproduction is a major life activity of respondent, I do not agree that an asymptomatic HIV infection "substantially limits" that activity. The record before us leaves no doubt that those so infected are still entirely able to engage in sexual intercourse, give birth to a child if they become pregnant, and perform the manual tasks necessary to rear a child to maturity. While individuals infected with HIV may choose not to engage in these activities, there is no support in language, logic, or our case law for the proposition that such voluntary choices constitute a "limit" on one's own life activities.

* * * Respondent contends that her ability to reproduce is limited because "the fatal nature of HIV infection means that a parent is unlikely to live long enough to raise and nurture the child to adulthood." But the ADA's definition of a disability is met only if the alleged impairment substantially "limits" (present tense) a major life activity. Asymptomatic HIV does not presently limit respondent's ability to perform any of the tasks necessary to bear or raise a child. Respondent's argument, taken to its logical extreme, would render every individual with a genetic marker for some debilitating disease "disabled" here and now because of some possible future effects.

In my view, therefore, respondent has failed to demonstrate that any of her major life activities were substantially limited by her HIV infection.

II

While the Court concludes to the contrary as to the "disability" issue, it then quite correctly recognizes that petitioner could nonetheless have refused to treat respondent if her condition posed a "direct threat." * * * I agree that the judgment should be vacated, although I am not sure I understand the Court's cryptic direction to the lower court.

* * * I agree with the Court that "the existence, or nonexistence, of a significant risk must be determined from the standpoint of the person who refuses the treatment or accommodation," as of the time that the decision refusing treatment is made. I disagree with the Court, however, that "[i]n assessing the reasonableness of petitioner's actions, the views of public health authorities . . . are of special weight and authority." Those views are, of course, entitled to a presumption of validity when the actions of those authorities themselves are challenged in court, and even in disputes between private parties where Congress has committed that dispute to adjudication by a public health authority. But in litigation between private parties originating in the federal courts, I am aware of no provision of law or judicial practice that would require or permit courts to give some scientific views more credence than others simply because they have been endorsed by a politically appointed public health authority (such as the Surgeon General). In litigation of this latter sort, which is what we face here, the credentials of the scientists employed by the public health authority, and the soundness of their studies, must stand on their own. The Court cites no authority for its limitation upon the courts' truth-finding function, except the statement in *School Bd. of Nassau Cty. v. Arline*, 480 U.S., at 288, that in making findings regarding the risk of contagion under the Rehabilitation Act, "courts normally should defer to the reasonable medical judgments of public health officials." But there is appended to that dictum the following footnote, which makes it very clear that the Court was urging respect for medical judgment, and not necessarily respect for "official" medical judgment over "private" medical judgment: "This case does not present, and we do not address, the question whether courts should also defer to the reasonable medical judgments of private physicians on which an employer has relied." *Id.*, at 288, n. 18.

* * * Given the "severity of the risk" involved here, i.e., near certain death, and the fact that no public health authority had outlined a protocol for eliminating this risk in the context of routine dental treatment, it seems likely that petitioner can establish that it was objectively reasonable for him to conclude that treating respondent in his office posed a "direct threat" to his safety. * * *

■ JUSTICE O'CONNOR, concurring in the judgment in part and dissenting in part.

I agree with the Chief Justice that respondent's claim of disability should be evaluated on an individualized basis and that she has not proven that her asymptomatic HIV status substantially limited one or more of her major life activities. In my view, the act of giving birth to a child, while a very important part of the lives of many women, is not generally the same as the representative major life activities of all persons—"caring for one's self, performing manual tasks, walking, seeing, hearing, speaking, breathing, learning, and working"—listed in regulations relevant to the Americans with Disabilities Act of 1990. Based on that conclusion, there is no need to address whether other aspects of intimate or family relationships not raised in this case could constitute major life activities; nor is there reason to consider whether HIV status would impose a substantial limitation on one's ability to reproduce if reproduction were a major life activity.

I join in Part II of the Chief Justice's opinion. * * *

Page 967—Insert after the *Anderson* decision:

Mark Cloutier v. Prudential Insurance Co.

United States District Court for the Northern District of California, 1997.
964 F.Supp. 299.

■ JUDGE WILLIAM H. ORRICK

* * * On February 8, 1995, plaintiff applied for an individual Variable Appreciable Life insurance policy from Prudential in the face amount of $500,000. With plaintiff's consent, Prudential reviewed his medical records, in accordance with its standard individual policy underwriting procedures. Those records revealed that plaintiff "has safe sex through [a] partner [who] is HIV [-positive]" and that plaintiff "has had persistently low CD–4 [white cell blood] count." The records also revealed an HIV-negative result in plaintiff's own blood test. Plaintiff attributes his low CD4 blood count to an unrelated bout with a viral infection many years ago, an assessment that Prudential apparently does not dispute.

[Prudential denied plaintiff a policy. During the same period, however, New York Life Insurance Company issued two individual life insurance policies to him; plaintiff alleged that he had revealed the same medical history to that company. Plaintiff sued for violation of the Americans with Disabilities Act. That statute prohibits discrimination in the "enjoyment of goods [and] services . . . by any place of public accommodation." The court finds that defendant's business of selling insurance falls within the meaning of "place of public accommodation." However, the ADA contains two special provisions regarding insurance. The first is a safe harbor: the ADA is not to be construed as prohibiting an insurer "from underwriting risks, classifying risks, or administering . . . risks." 42 U.S.C. 12202(c)(1). The second bars a defendant from relying on that safe harbor if such reliance constitutes a "subterfuge" to evade the purposes of the ADA in prohibiting workplace discrimination. *Id.* Plaintiff asserts that Prudential is engaged in such a subterfuge.]

* * * Borrowing from [the legislative history], the Court can fashion a legal standard by which to evaluate the [meaning of "subterfuge"]: insurers retain their § 501(c) exemption so long as their underwriting decisions are in accord with either (a) sound actuarial principles, or (b) actual or reasonably anticipated experience. Prudential alleges that it bases its underwriting practices on "medical principles establishing that, as a group, these individuals [who engage in sex with HIV-positive partners] present a greater risk of becoming infected with HIV ... than does a group where neither sexual partner is HIV-positive." Assuming that Prudential rejected plaintiff's policy application on this basis alone—as the Court must in the absence of any additional evidence—Prudential views the issue too narrowly. The mere fact that a particular individual presents a greater risk does not compel the conclusion that the individual presents an uninsurable risk. Common sense suggests that an insurer that confronts a heterogenous pool of applicants merely consults actuarial tables to adjust its rates to account for varying levels of risk presented by those applicants. Indeed, Prudential's practices typically conform with this logic, as the company admits that it charges about 10 percent of its applicants a premium commensurate with the additional risk that those applicants bring to its pool. Yet Prudential offers no actuarial or other data to justify its outright rejection of plaintiff's policy application. As one court noted in a case involving an insurer's rejection of an AIDS-afflicted plaintiff in the group life insurance context:

> The ADA explicitly allows some disability-based distinctions within insurance policies to be drawn by insurers. However, total denial of ... coverage to an individual does not implicate risks. In other words, disability-based distinctions are only relevant when some coverage is extended to an individual with disabilities. No actuarial risk makes someone uninsurable.

Anderson v. Gus Mayer Boston Store, 924 F. Supp. 763, 779 (E.D.Tex. 1996) (footnote omitted). Although the instant dispute involves the refusal to issue individual coverage, as opposed to the extension of group coverage to an individual, *Anderson*'s logic applies with equal force here. More important, Prudential does not point to any specific evidence to support this assertion. It argues that it need not offer specific actuarial data to support its decision where it seems so obviously supported by "accepted medical principles" and common knowledge about AIDS and its associated mortality risks. The Court disagrees. Though Prudential can meet its initial burden as a Rule 56 movant without presenting evidence that negates plaintiff's claim, plaintiff has demonstrated the existence of a material dispute as to whether Prudential based its decision upon sound actuarial principles or reasonably anticipated experience. In response to plaintiff's showing, Prudential must point to data, studies, or other information relevant to its risk assessment in order to establish the absence of a dispute of material fact.

Specifically, plaintiff discharged his burden by pointing to deposition testimony from Prudential underwriters who "admitted that they either did not recall seeking or definitely did not seek information outside of their own knowledge regarding HIV. None of them recalled specifics of any special training relating to HIV or its transmission, and only one of them had any medical training."Plaintiff further asserts that none of the key Prudential employees "consulted medical literature, epidemiological experts, or even in-house actuaries," in deciding to reject plaintiff's application. Plaintiff also points to the declaration of Harry Woodman, a former Chief Underwriter at New York Life, with forty-six years of underwriting experience. Woodman alleges that "in order to make a decision based on sound actuarial reasoning and on a legitimate basis, Prudential should have evaluated [plaintiff's] actual risk of contracting HIV before making a final decision on his application." (Woodman concludes that he would have offered plaintiff an insurance policy had he been confronted with the same application).

Not only does the evidence suggest that Prudential did not base its decision on sound actuarial data, but the rejection of his application may not have accorded with reasonably anticipated experience. Prudential's review of plaintiff's medical records could only have revealed that plaintiff engaged in "safe sex"—that is, protected sex—with an HIV-positive partner. Plaintiff's blood test results remained HIV-negative. Despite that fact, Prudential does not offer any evidence that one has a heightened risk, let alone a uninsurable risk, of contracting HIV by engaging in protected sex. Persons such as plaintiff, who took the initiative to report the nature of his sexual activity to his doctor, could conceivably have a lower likelihood of contracting the virus than someone who does not regularly see a doctor, does not seek medical advice, and does not purport to take precautions before engaging in sexual activity.

Of course, plaintiff could become infected with the HIV virus in spite of his apparent precautions. In Prudential's most specific allegation on the topic, its Director of Medical Services, Dr. Amy Bennett, states that "because the HIV retrovirus becomes incorporated into the genome of the host's immune cells, it is extremely difficult to develop antiviral chemotherapeutic agents or vaccines to eradicate the disease." But the medical profession need not eradicate the disease to enable HIV-infected persons to enjoy a life of a reasonably lengthy duration. As Woodman notes, the recent development of antiviral drugs and other medications have enabled persons who contract the HIV virus to live another twenty-five years after exposure. In particular, the recent use of protease inhibitors in combination with other antiviral treatments has reduced the presence of the HIV virus to undetectable levels in some patients.

If one can live many years after infection, such persons as plaintiff hardly present uninsurable risks for a life insurance company. New York Life's decision to issue plaintiff two individual policies in 1996, in spite of New York Life's full knowledge of plaintiff's sexual activities, bolsters this conclusion.

In light of the conflicting evidence, Prudential can only prevail if it provides the Court with facts sufficiently specific to convince the Court of an absence of disputed fact. The Court does not stand alone in demanding such a showing, as revealed by other courts that have addressed the question in the context of HIV-infected insurance applicants. *Anderson*, 924 F. Supp. at 779, and *Piquard v. City of East Peoria*, 887 F. Supp. 1106, 1125–26 (C.D.Ill.1995). In *Anderson*, the court ruled against the defendant where its insurer "made no claim that it has conducted any . . . studies." In the context of an employer-sponsored group benefit plan, the court further opined that the ADA "puts the burden on those actors classifying risks to show both their rationality and permissibility." In *Piquard*, also a benefit plan case, the court required that an employer or the employer's insurer bear the burden of providing "risk assessment and actuarial data" to prevail on summary judgment. * * *

It defies the spirit of the ADA for the Court to accept Prudential's proffer of vague explanations of the risks of HIV infection where the business of insurance requires sound risk assessment practices. Because plaintiff has pointed to evidence revealing the possibility of discriminatory denial of an insurance policy, Prudential can only prevail on summary judgment by coming forward with actuarial or other data supporting its actions.* * *

Postscript- After the denial of summary judgment, the parties settled the case. 1997 U.S.Dist. LEXIS 8788 (N.D.Cal.1997).

*

CHAPTER 11

The Law's Construction of Consent

SECTION 1

Forcible Sex

PART A. THE LAW OF RAPE

Page 981—Add the following note:

4. *Rape and Other Laws Criminalizing Consensual Sex.* If the sexual encounter at issue in *Rusk* was not rape, then what was it, legally? Adultery or fornication, depending on the marital status of the persons involved, i.e., still a crime in many states. Framed another way, Pat was either a victim of rape or a perpetrator of adultery (she was separated from her husband when the crime occurred, 424 A.2d at 721). Using *Rusk* as an example, Professor Anne Coughlin argues that one reason judges such as dissenting Judge Cole may have so harshly assessed the woman's testimony was that, if the act was not rape, she was herself guilty of a crime. In this way, the criminalization of non-marital heterosexual conduct silently structures rape law by positioning the victims as "defendants who seek to be excused from criminal liability . . . [W]e might even advance the proposition that courts were not treating rape victims *differently from* other crime victims, but rather were treating them *the same as* other crime perpetrators who pleaded for an excuse." Anne M. Coughlin, "Sex and Guilt," 84 *Va. L. Rev.* 1, 41 (1998) (emphasis in the original).

Page 995–Insert the following at the end of Problem 11–2:

The courts remain split on the constitutionality of VAWA. A panel of the Fourth Circuit reversed the district court's dismissal of the complaint in *Brzonkala*, but the full circuit then granted rehearing *en banc. Brzonkala v. Virginia Polytechnic Institute and State University*, No. 96–1814 (Feb. 5, 1998) (unpublished), *vacating* 132 F.3d 949 (4th Cir.1997).

PART C. SADOMASOCHISM: "CONSENSUAL VIOLENCE"?

Page 1010–Add to Note on the "Spanner" case:

The European Court of Human Rights affirmed the decision in the casebook. The European court ruled that the British House of Lords decision did not violate Article 8 of the European Convention on Human Rights, which protects "respect for . . . private life." *Laskey, Jaggard and Brown v. United Kingdom*, 24 E.H.H.R. 39 (1997). "[T]he state is unquestionably entitled to regulate, through the operation of the criminal law, activities which involve the infliction of physical harm." *Id*. at 58. The court also found that determination of the tolerable level of harm where the victim consented was primarily a matter for the state's authorities. The court found no anti-gay bias, and concluded that the decision was based "on the extreme nature of the practices." *Id*. at 59.

CHAPTER 12

THE BODY: NEW FRONTIERS

SECTION 1

AIDS: THE CONFLATION OF SEXUALITY AND DISEASE

PART B. PUBLIC HEALTH LAW

Page 1090–Add to the end of Note 2:

In *Bragdon v. Abbott*, 118 S.Ct. 2196 (1998) (excerpt appears in Chapter 10, Section 3C of this Supplement, pp. 132–42), the Supreme Court clarified that HIV disease is a disability within the meaning of the ADA even in early, asymptomatic stages. The Court also reviewed whether the lower courts had properly granted summary judgment to the plaintiff, an HIV-infected woman who was refused dental care, on the question of whether the defendant was justified in setting special conditions for providing the care because there was a "direct threat" (the defense allowed by the ADA) to him in treating her. The Court ruled that only information proven to be available to defendant at the time of the incident could be considered, and directed the court of appeals to take into consideration CDC reports of seven dental workers who had become infected for reasons unknown at the time defendant refused to treat plaintiff. The Court held that, although the views of public health authorities such as CDC are "of special weight and authority," they are not conclusive. "A health care professional who disagrees with the prevailing consensus may refute it by citing a credible scientific basis for deviating from the accepted norm." *Id.* at 16.

149

Transgender Issues and the Law

Page 1117—Add following the Note:

Tasha S. Maggert v. Craig A. Hanks, et al.

United States Court of Appeals for the Seventh Circuit, 1997.
131 F.3d 670.

■ Chief Judge Posner.

A prisoner appeals from the dismissal of a suit in which he claims that the prison's failure to give him estrogen therapy for a psychiatric condition known technically as gender dysphoria and more popularly as transsexualism is a form of cruel and unusual punishment. A psychiatrist hired by the prison on a contract basis refused to prescribe estrogen for the prisoner, Maggert, instead recommending that he continue to see the prison psychologist for counseling.

The judge was clearly right to dismiss the suit. The psychiatrist does not believe that Maggert suffers from gender dysphoria, although he acknowledges that Maggert's "sexual identity is polymorphous and his sexual aims ambiguous." Maggert has not submitted a contrary affidavit by a qualified expert and so has not created a genuine issue of material fact that would keep this case alive.

But there is a broader issue, having to do with the significance of gender dysphoria in prisoners' civil rights litigation, that we want to address. Although gender dysphoria is a rare condition, it has been invoked in enough prisoner cases to give rise to the term "the jurisprudence of transsexualism." Debra Sherman Tedeschi, "The Predicament of the Transsexual Prisoner," 5 *Temple Polit. & Civ. Rts. L.Rev. 27* (1995). The problematic character of this jurisprudence arises from the following considerations. The Eighth Amendment has been interpreted to forbid prisons to ignore the serious medical, including psychiatric, afflictions of prisoners. Gender dysphoria—the condition in which a person believes that he is imprisoned in a body of the wrong sex, that though biologically a male (the more common form of the condition) he is "really" a female—is a serious psychiatric disorder, as we know because the people afflicted by it will go to great lengths to cure it if they can afford the cure. The cure for the male transsexual consists not of psychiatric treatment designed to make the patient content with his biological sexual identity—that doesn't work—but of estrogen therapy designed to create the secondary sexual characteristics of a woman followed by the surgical removal of the genitals and the construction of a vagina-substitute out of penile tissue. Someone eager to undergo this mutilation is plainly suffering from a profound psychiatric disorder.

Does it follow that prisons have a duty to administer (if the prisoner requests it) the standard cure to a prisoner who unlike Maggert is diagnosed as a genuine transsexual? The cases do not answer "yes," but they make the question easier than it really is by saying that the choice of treatment is up to the prison. The implication is that less drastic (and, not incidentally, less costly) treatments are available for this condition. However, we have found only one report of successful nonradical treatment of gender dysphoria. [citation omitted]

Yet it does not follow that the prisons have a duty to authorize the hormonal and surgical procedures that in most cases at least would be necessary to "cure" a prisoner's gender dysphoria. Those procedures are protracted and expensive. Even after a person is diagnosed as having gender dysphoria, treatment protocols require that he complete at least three months of psychotherapy before beginning to take estrogen, and that before undergoing the surgical last stage of the treatment he live for two or three years in the "gender of orientation" while taking estrogen; during this period nongenital surgeries and electrolysis are performed as part of the treatment. A prison is not required by the Eighth Amendment to give a prisoner medical care that is as good as he would receive if he were a free person, let alone an affluent free person. He is entitled only to minimum care. Although some cases hold that states cannot categorically exclude sex-change operations from Medicaid coverage, many state Medicaid statutes contain a blanket exclusion, and we imagine that as a practical matter it is extremely difficult to obtain Medicaid reimbursement for such a procedure. In general, then, you have to pay for the treatment yourself; and the total cost, which can easily reach $100,000, puts the treatment beyond the reach of a person of average wealth. Withholding from a prisoner an esoteric medical treatment that only the wealthy can afford does not strike us as a form of cruel and unusual punishment. It is not unusual; and we cannot see what is cruel about refusing a benefit to a person who could not have obtained the benefit if he had refrained from committing crimes. We do not want transsexuals committing crimes because it is the only route to obtaining a cure.

It is not the cost *per se* that drives this conclusion. For life-threatening or crippling conditions, Medicaid and other public-aid, insurance, and charity programs authorize treatments that often exceed $100,000. Gender dysphoria is not, at least not yet, generally considered a severe enough condition to warrant expensive treatment at the expense of others than the person suffering from it. That being so, making the treatment a constitutional duty of prisons would give prisoners a degree of medical care that they could not obtain if they obeyed the law.

We conclude that, except in special circumstances that we do not at present foresee, the Eighth Amendment does not entitle a prison inmate to curative treatment for his gender dysphoria. Of course, as the cases have already established, he is entitled to be protected, by assignment to protective custody or otherwise, from harassment by prisoners who wish to use him as a sexual plaything, provided that the danger is both acute and known to the authorities. E.g., *Farmer v. Brennan*, 511 U.S. 825, 833–34 (1994)

Page 1124. Substitute the following for, or read it in connection with,
    Farmer:

Michelle Murray v. United States Bureau of Prisons, et al.

United States Court of Appeals for the Sixth Circuit, 1997.
106 F.3d 401 (unpublished) (Table).

■ PER CURIAM.

At all times relevant to this action, Michelle Murray was both a biologically male transsexual and a federal prisoner. Although she has undergone extensive hormone therapy, has had breast implants, and has been castrated, she remains anatomically male. Accordingly, the United States Bureau of Prisons has assigned her to male prisons for incarceration. * * *

The claims on which the magistrate judge awarded summary judgment to the defendants are divisible into six categories. First, Murray alleges that on several occasions prison officials have violated her rights by placing her in segregated confinement, in some cases ostensibly for her own safety and in other cases as punishment for her violations of orders to wear a brassiere. Second, she claims that she is entitled to receive hair and skin products that are necessary for her to maintain a feminine appearance. Third, she claims that prison officials have repeatedly harassed her verbally, disparaging her for her status as a transsexual and for what they presume to be her sexual preference. Fourth, she alleges three separate instances of physical abuse by prison officials. Fifth, she claims that the prison's physician, Dr. Lusito Benin, exhibited deliberate indifference to her medical needs by failing to return the dosage of her estrogen treatments to the level that she had received when she first became a federal prisoner. Finally, she alleges that prison officials wrote up a false incident report in retaliation for the filing of her original complaint in this action. We discuss each set of claims in turn, mindful that our review of an award of summary judgment is de novo, and that in order to prevail the defendants below must show that, viewing the evidence in the light most favorable to the plaintiff, no rational fact-finder could return a verdict in her favor.

A.   Segregated Confinement

While at FCI Ashland, Murray was placed in segregated confinement on several occasions. The defendants argue that the first two such occasions were justified in order to protect Murray from assault by other inmates. She was first placed in segregation on June 16, 1993, the day that she arrived at FCI Ashland, and was held there for six days until the warden approved her placement into the general population. Shortly thereafter, she was assaulted by an inmate, and she was again placed in segregation on June 25 for twelve days during the pendency of the investigation into the attack.

The magistrate judge held that neither placement stated a constitutional claim, and we agree. With respect to the first placement, the defendants certainly acted within the bounds established by either the Eighth Amendment or the Due Process Clause of the Fifth Amendment in segregating Murray until they could determine whether she would be safe in the general population; indeed, they may have subjected themselves to an Eighth Amendment claim if they had failed to do so. The defendants' concerns are borne out by the fact that an attack did, in fact, occur after Murray's release from segregation. With respect to the second placement, the defendants had a valid interest in protecting Murray both from retaliation for reporting the assault and from attempts to dissuade her from testifying at a disciplinary proceeding.

All of Murray's subsequent instances of segregated confinement arose as penalties for her repeated refusal to obey orders to wear a brassiere. Murray objects that the orders were improper. The magistrate judge held that the orders were reasonable efforts to maintain institutional order and security, and that, since there was no evidence that the orders constituted an exaggerated response to those considerations, he was required to defer to the expert judgment of prison officials on this matter.* * * The orders to wear a brassiere were valid; therefore, the defendants properly placed Murray in segregated confinement for her failure to obey those orders.

B.   Hair and Skin Products

Murray alleges that, while she was at FCI Morgantown, she was provided with hair and skin products that she claims are necessary for her to maintain a feminine appearance. Murray claims that the failure of prison officials at FCI Ashland to continue that practice violates the Eighth Amendment. The magistrate judge applied *Hudson v. McMillian*, 503 U.S.

1 (1992), to hold that these deprivations do not state a constitutional claim. That holding is correct: "Because routine discomfort is part of the penalty that criminal offenders pay for their offenses against society, only those deprivations denying the minimal civilized measure of life's necessities are sufficiently grave to form the basis of an Eighth Amendment violation." 503 U.S. at 9 (internal quotations omitted). Cosmetic products are not among the minimal civilized measure of life's necessities.

C.   Verbal Harassment

Murray alleges that numerous prison officials repeatedly have made offensive remarks to her with regard to her bodily appearance, her transsexualism, and her presumed sexual preference. The magistrate judge correctly held that verbal abuse cannot state an Eighth Amendment claim. If Murray's allegations are true, the behavior of the prison officials was certainly not commendable. Although we do not condone the alleged statements, the Eighth Amendment does not afford us the power to correct every action, statement, or attitude of a prison official with which we might disagree.

D.   Physical Abuse

Murray alleges that prison officials abused her on three separate occasions. [The first claim went to trial, and the jury found for the defendant.] * * *

In the second claim, Murray alleges that, on August 28, 1993, Officer Billy Caudill and an unidentified officer approached her in the prison cafeteria, Caudill made an insulting comment regarding her breasts, and the other officer subjected her to a pat-down search during which he unnecessarily touched her breasts. Murray has sued only Caudill, and not the unidentified officer. * * * There is no allegation that the pat-down search was improper, that Caudill directed the other officer either to search Murray or to touch her breasts, or that the touch lasted long enough that Caudill could have acted to stop it. Under these circumstances, Caudill is not liable for the other officer's actions.

Murray's third claim arises from her placement in segregated confinement on September 6, 1993, for her failure to comply with an order to wear a brassiere. Officer William Underwood searched her before taking her to her new quarters. Murray alleges that, during the course of the search, Officer Underwood kicked her legs apart, causing her to lose her balance and fall. That kick does not state a constitutional claim. * * * "The undisputed facts show that Underwood did not kick Murray because of malice or sadism, but because the kick was reasonably thought to be necessary to complete the pat-down search."

E.   Deliberate Indifference to Medical Needs

The policy of the Bureau of Prisons is to provide a transsexual prisoner with the level of female hormones necessary to ensure that she neither progresses nor regresses in the development of feminine attributes. Murray alleges that, when she first entered the federal prison system at FCI Springfield, Missouri, a mistake was made and that she received a prescription for a lower dosage of female hormones than that which she had received previously in the outside world. Murray alleges that the mistake was repeated both at FCI Morgantown and at FCI Ashland. She further alleges that the Chief of Health Services at FCI Ashland, Dr. Lusito Benin, has refused to increase her dosage despite being informed of the error. Under these facts, Murray has failed to state a constitutional claim. Since transsexualism is a recognized medical disorder, and transsexuals often have a serious medical need for some sort of treatment, a complete refusal by prison officials to provide a transsexual with any treatment at all would state an Eighth Amendment claim for deliberate indifference to medical needs. However, where, as here, the prisoner is receiving treatment, the dosage levels of which are based on the considered professional judgment of a physician, we are reluctant to second-guess that judgment.* * *

F.   Retaliation

After Murray filed her initial complaint in this matter, on the morning of May 14, 1994, Correctional Officer Bryan Miller discovered her in her cell in bed with another inmate, and issued an incident report against Murray. Later that day, Murray was placed in segregated confinement pending the investigation of the charge. Lieutenant John Jones took Murray's statement; in that statement, Murray alleged that the inmate was only sitting on the edge of her bed, and that Officer Miller told her that he would not issue the report if she agreed to dismiss the complaint. On May 25, 1994, Disciplinary Hearing Officer Sam Biafore conducted Murray's hearing and found her guilty of "attempting to engage in sexual activity." Biafore specifically stated that he found Officer Miller's version of events to be more credible than Murray's. Accordingly, he imposed a penalty of fifteen days in segregation. [The court found that evidence in the record supported the disciplinary action and denied relief to the plaintiff.] * * *

†